THE PENGUIN ATLAS
OF DIASPORAS

THE PENGUIN ATLAS OF DIASPORAS

by

Gérard Chaliand and Jean-Pierre Rageau

Maps by Catherine Petit

Translated from the French by A. M. Berrett

VIKING

VIKING
Published by the Penguin Group
Penguin Books USA Inc., 375 Hudson Street, New York, New York 10014, U.S.A.
Penguin Books Ltd, 27 Wrights Lane, London W8 5TZ, England
Penguin Books Australia Ltd, Ringwood, Victoria, Australia
Penguin Books Canada Ltd, 10 Alcorn Avenue, Toronto, Ontario, Canada M4V 3B2
Penguin Books (N.Z.) Ltd, 182-190 Wairau Road, Auckland 10, New Zealand

Penguin Books Ltd, Registered Offices:
Harmondsworth, Middlesex, England

First published in 1995 by Viking Penguin, a division of Penguin Books USA Inc.

1 3 5 7 9 10 8 6 4 2

Translation copyright © Gerard Chaliand and Jean-Pierre Rageau, 1995
All rights reserved

Originally published in France as *Atlas des Diasporas* by Editions Odile Jacob. © Editions Odile Jacob, 1991.

LIBRARY OF CONGRESS CATALOGING IN PUBLICATION DATA
Chaliand, Gérard.
[Atlas des diasporas. English]
The Penguin atlas of the diasporas/by Gerard Chaliand and Jean-Pierre Rageau; maps by Catherine Petit; translated from the French by A.M. Barrett.
p. cm.
Includes bibliographical references.
Contents: the problem of diasporas—The Jewish diaspora—The Armenian diaspora—The Gypsy diaspora—The Black diaspora—The Chinese diaspora—The Indian diaspora—The Irish diaspora—The Greek diaspora—The Lebanese diaspora—The Palestinian diaspora—The Vietnamese and Korean diasporas.
ISBN 0-670-85439-5
1.Man—Migrations—Atlases. 2. Migrations of nations—Atlases. I. Rageau, Jean-Pierre. II. Title. III. Title: Atlas of the diasporas.
GN370.C43   1995
304.8—dc20   94–20640

This book is printed on acid-free paper.

Printed in the United States of America
Set in Times New Roman

Le Tybre seul, qui vers la mer s´enfuit,
　Reste de Rome. O mondaine inconstance!
Ce qui est ferme, est par le temps destruit,
Et ce qui fuit, au temps fait resistance.

—Joachim du Bellay
Antiquitez de Rome (1558)

Ne ought save *Tyber* hastning to his fall
Remaines of all. O worlds inconstancie!
　That which is firme doth flit and fall away,
　And that is flitting, doth abide and stay.

—translated by Edmund Spenser

ACKNOWLEDGMENTS

Attempting to prepare an atlas of diasporas is a challenge, as the difficulties are numerous, not the least of which is the very definition of the term "diaspora" and, consequently, of the peoples who may be treated as diaspora peoples. In most cases the sources are spotty, and often they are totally lacking.

Off the beaten track, our task has not been easy and we are conscious of the exploratory nature of what we have undertaken. But such as it is, we hope our work has the merit of opening up an area that has been too long neglected.

We would like to thank Rachael Ertel for kindly agreeing to look over the section of our work devoted to the Jewish diaspora; Gérard Libaridian for the section dealing with the Armenians, and Léon Poliakov for his valuable advice.

CONTENTS

▲ This scroll of Esther epitomizes the complexity of the diasporic phenomenon. Why, if it was crafted in a Jewish Levantine community or in a Jewish community along the Mediterranean, probably circa 1700, is the Hebrew text adorned with Chinese miniatures? At its time of manufacture, about three hundred Jewish families lived in Kaifeng, capital of the Chinese province of Henan (Photo © J.-L. Charmet).

INTRODUCTION:
THE PROBLEM OF
DIASPORAS

There is no ambiguity about the term *diaspora*[1]—"dispersion"—when it is used in relation to the Jewish people.[2] But once it is applied to other religious or ethnic groups, it becomes immediately apparent how difficult it is in many cases to find a definition that makes a clear distinction between a migration and a diaspora, or between a minority and a diaspora.

Thus the term "diaspora" is not used when discussing the presence of descendants of British people in Australia, New Zealand, South Africa, Zimbabwe, Kenya, Canada, and the United States. Nor is the term applied to the many German colonies established in central and eastern Europe as far as the Volga (all but vanished since 1945), nor in several Latin American countries. These latter colonies may often have emigrated several generations ago, but, in both Chile and Argentina, for instance, they continue to retain their identity—a key feature of diasporas. The geographer Pierre George has used the judicious expression "minorities of superiority"[3] to refer to them, meaning minorities that wish to perpetuate their identity, which they see as culturally superior.

Conversely, and making matters even more complex, there is a widespread tendency to apply the term "diaspora" to the Chinese and Indian communities scattered across the globe when European imperialism was at its height in the second half of the nineteenth century, in southeast Asia, the West Indies, the Indian Ocean, eastern and southern Africa, and the United States. These groups ought indeed to be classified as diasporas (or perhaps *semi-diasporas*, given the continued existence of a state where the vast majority of their compatriots live), insofar as they meet many of the criteria that define the diaspora condition.

1. The Greek word *diaspora* is used by Thucydides (*Peloponnesian War,* II, 27) to describe the exile of the population of Aegina. The Hebrew word *galut (Deuteronomy,* 28:25) was employed to refer to the forced exile of the Jews in Babylon (586 B.C.) The word was later used in the sense of dispersion to describe the Christian communities scattered across the Roman Empire before it adopted Christianity as the state religion.

2. Richard Marienstras, *Etre un peuple en diaspora*, preface by Pierre Vidal-Naquet, (Paris: Maspéro, 1975).

3. Pierre George, *Géopolitique des minorités (Paris: P.U.F. 1983).* One could also speak of "minorites of inferiorization." This is the case, for example, with the Korean minorities in Japan, often established for several generations (see below).

What then are the criteria which taken separately or together constitute the specific fact of a diaspora?

1. A diaspora is defined as *the collective forced dispersion of a religious and/or ethnic group,* precipitated by a disaster, often of a political nature.

Yet, if we are to include in this definition cases other than that of the Jews and the Armenians, for example, we must include other models and causes.

What of the Gypsy diaspora? Originally from northern India, the Gypsies migrated to the Middle East in the ninth to tenth centuries and subsequently spread throughout Europe—from Spain to Russia. But it has never been shown that their migration was political in origin, or consequent upon a natural disaster.

Shouldn't the millions of African slaves deported during the seventeenth to nineteenth centuries—a forced dispersion which covered almost the whole of the American continent, from the United States to Brazil by way of the West Indies and the countries of the Caribbean—constitute a diaspora?[4] But the blacks taken from Africa were not a people, a homogeneous population, unlike other groups that form a diaspora, which have more in common than their misfortune and the color of their skin. They came from tribes with different languages and traditions, whom the slavers generally took care to mix up, to reduce the group cohesion of their cargo. Moreover, the slaves were sold and not grouped together as they would have wished. Thus their "collective baggage" was destroyed or atomized.

Is there an Irish diaspora?[5] Their departures in large numbers in the sec-

4. Joseph E. Harris, *Global Dimensions of the African Diaspora* (Washington, D.C.: Howard University Press, 1982).

5. See "Géopolitique des minorities," *Hérodote* 53 (April-May 1989).

ond half of the nineteenth century were the result of economic causes (famine, for example), and more of them left their country than stayed. Yet the case of the Irish is not unique in the world. The Cape Verdeans, for example, find themselves in a similar situation: the majority of them are in the United States and Portugal. For the Irish as for the Cape Verdeans it remains an open question *whether we are dealing with a migration or a dispersion.* Can we speak of dispersion when the overwhelming majority of migrants have gone to a single country, or indeed two or three countries, often linguistically similar to their home country?

The dispersion of the Chinese and Indian communities, comparable in sheer numbers, who set out at the same time and for similar reasons (hunger, extreme poverty), is far more extensive geographically, covering as it does all five continents. More than ten million Chinese[6] and Indians left regions ravaged by famines, epidemics, and conflicts, thereby constituting semi-diasporas.

2. A diaspora is also defined by the role played by *collective memory, which transmits both the historical facts that precipitated the dispersion and a cultural heritage (broadly understood)*—the latter often being religious.

This collective memory is especially vivid among peoples who have suffered a disaster: the genocide of the Armenians in the Ottoman Empire (about half the Armenian population was wiped out in 1915–1916; the ancient exiles of the Jews and their genocide during the Second World War; the Palestinians dispossessed of their land by the Arab-Israeli war. The Gypsies, an oral society, may not have transcribed their memories of Nazi genocide, but to believe that such an occurrence has been forgotten because it has not

6. Mention should also be made of the long-term presence of trading colonies (Chinese, Greek, Armenian, etc.) often described today as trading diasporas.

been written down would be to underestimate the capacity for a continuing oral transmission.

In the case of African-Americans a significant part of their heritage has been re-created or syncretized.[7] Sometimes even the African diaspora, or at least part of its elite, has endeavoured to reconstruct it, with a mythical projection into a Pharaonic, biblical, or Ethiopian past. Such is the case with the "return" to Liberia in 1822 and with the subsequent development in the United States of ideas of a return to Africa, as propounded by Marcus Garvey in the early twentieth century. In Brazil there were less spectacular cases of a "return" to Benin or Nigeria.

Reference should also be made to smaller-scale diasporas such as that of the Assyro-Chaldaeans,[8] as it is often small peoples that are defeated and scatter. Heirs to a long tradition, as their name indicates, they have been twice driven out of the lands they occupied in this century: first as a Christian minority in the Ottoman Empire during the First World War and a second time in Iraq in the 1930s.

3. Even more important among the factors that go to make up a diaspora is the group's will to transmit its heritage in order to preserve its identity, whatever the degree of integration. What characterizes a diaspora, as much as its spatial dispersion, is *the will to survive as a minority by transmitting a heritage.*

In this respect, the religious factor is in the long run more or less important. It is fundamental[9] in the case of the Jews, and essential for the Armenians in a non-Christian environment, but secondary for the Gypsies, whose way of life and language play a more decisive role. For a century and

7. Roger Bastide, *African Civilizations in the New World,* trans. Peter Green (London: C. Hurst, 1971).

8. Joseph Yacoub, *Les Assyro-Chaldéens* (Paris: Groupement pour les droits des minorités, 1986).

9. Although not indispensable: cf. the concept of "Spinozan Jew" (E. Morin).

a half, the Chinese and Indian (both Hindu and Muslim) diasporas have transmitted a culture and a religion that have remained for the most part very much alive, no matter the country they're found in.

There is always part of a diaspora that assimilates and disappears. While the Lebanese diaspora in sub-Saharan Africa today fully retains its own characteristics, the first Lebanese diaspora, now settled in Brazil and Argentina or the United States for about a century, is tending to lose its specific features. In general, the closer the host culture is in terms of religion, and the more democratic its institutions, the more probable a diaspora's progressive dilution and even assimilation.

Given the religious factor, there is nothing surprising in the fact that the Jews have maintained their customary ways through the vicissitudes of history. For the same reasons, the descendants of Armenians deported in the seventeenth century to Iran have retained their identity. Blacks in the United States and Brazil, especially after the abolition of slavery, have sought equality and consequently the greatest possible integration. It is the obstacles put in the way of such integration that have led some black American or West Indian elites to glorify their African past and the myth of return.

The last variable affecting a diaspora's survival is numbers. Groups that are too small or too isolated tend to dissolve.

4. Finally, then, what in the last analysis makes it possible to assert that a given group is or is not a diaspora is *the time factor*. Only time decides whether a minority that meets all or some of the criteria described above, having insured its survival and adaptation, is a diaspora.

The history of the last few centuries is full of examples of groups which, having partly emigrated, have blended into a different set of people. Thus Poles and Italians have assimilated into the population of France, the leading host country on the European continent. In the United States, the white minorities (over 35 million immigrants between 1850 and 1914) have almost all blended into the American nation. The future will determine whether such groups that are today dispersed will be able or want to form diasporas. This *desire to endure* as an exiled or transplanted and dispersed group is achieved through a network of associations and communications.[10] These networks ensure dynamism and fluidity; they are local but at the same time cross the boundaries of states.

Like other historical formations, diasporas form and disappear. This was the case with the Greeks. Under Rome and during the Hellenistic period the Greeks experienced both an intellectual and a trading dispersion. After the fall of Constantinople another dispersion—notably in Italy—occurred. Finally, Greek colonies survived until quite recently in Asia Minor: those in Pontus, deported and massacred during the First World War, and those in the Aegean, expelled and exchanged for Muslims in 1922, when the Turkish republic was founded. (About 1.2 million Greek Christians were expelled and exchanged for some 650,000 Turkish Muslims.) Another part of this very ancient diaspora ceased to exist in Alexandria with the advent of Nasserism; the poet Constantine Cavafy in this century was its most illustrious representative.

Jews, Armenians, and Greeks have formed long-lasting diasporas, a specific feature of which was that they were trading and hence urban ones.

10. Such a network is admirably described, for example, in the case of the Chinese diaspora in southeast Asia by Eric Ambler in *Passage of Arms* (London: Fontana, 1959).

Economic and cultural backwardness in relation to the host society is not, generally, the distinctive feature of ancient diasporas. In this respect, the Gypsies are an exception. The dispersion of blacks through slavery and the slave trade is more recent. Even more recent are other diasporas or semi-diasporas that stretch from the mid-nineteenth century (Chinese, Indians) to 1975–1990 for the latest, the Vietnamese. While that makes it difficult to assess such diasporas, we may, however, already observe their determination to transmit a cultural and linguistic heritage—that is, to survive as minorities in their host country.

For this *Atlas* we have restricted ourselves to the history of the principal diasporas and semi-diasporas.[11] In our approach, and given what has been said above, we have not sought to make a sharp distinction between "authentic" diasporas and those whose status may be disputed. Is there or is there not, strictly speaking, a black diaspora? Should the Palestinians be seen as being in a diaspora or (at least in the case of those who live along the Jordan and could become citizens of a future Palestinian state) in temporary exile? Do the Irish constitute a diaspora or rather a migration? Is it right to establish a link between the Armenian diasporas of old and the massive one that occurred following the genocide of 1915? And so on.

For many reasons, therefore, our final choices may rouse debate: Jews, Armenians, Gypsies, blacks, Chinese, Indians, Irish, Greeks, Lebanese, Palestinians, Vietnamese, and Koreans. For example, among the semi-diasporas, we might have taken the case of the Japanese, who like their Chinese contemporaries (from 1885 to the ban on Asian immigration in 1924), and similarly driven by need, left their country in large numbers.

11. See Gabriel Sheffen, ed., *Modern Diasporas in International Politics* (London: Croom Helm, 1986).

Japanese emigration was initially to Hawaii, where the sugar plantations offered jobs. After the American annexation of Hawaii, it shifted to California. During the Second World War, the Japanese minorities, naturalized or not, who were settled along the Pacific coast of the United States and Canada were interned in concentration camps because the authorities saw them as a potential "fifth column"; it was not until 1986 that these communities received an official apology from the United States and Canada for the treatment inflicted on them at that time. There is still a large Japanese community in Latin America. But since the end of the Second World War Japanese emigration has effectively ceased; the Japanese settled in east Asia during the period 1910–1945 returned to Japan.

The case of the Koreans is more complicated. A quite old emigration exists in Japan (400,000 in 1930), where it continues to be treated as an inferiorized minority. Small colonies exist in Sakhalin and in eastern Siberia, without so far having had the possibility of returning to Korea. Above all, over the last twenty years, a continuing movement of emigration has led more than 800,000 Koreans to the United States. But can we speak of a Korean dispersion, when it is essentially concentrated in two countries, and lacks the massive character of, say, the Irish migration? Conversely, the Vietnamese case, born of particular political conditions and fueled by terrible impoverishment, is a dispersion in all directions.

Finally, it is interesting to observe[12] that several states have been created by diaspora communities over the last two centuries: Haiti, Liberia, Israel, Singapore, Cape Verde. Various other small states, often islands, are essentially made up of dispersed communities: Trinidad, Surinam, Guiana, Mauritius,[13] etc.

12. See K. Tölöyan, *Diasporas,* (Middletown, CT: Wesleyan University Press, 1987).

13. In earlier times, the Sultanate of Zanzibar was created by trading colonies from southern Arabia.

One cannot fail to be struck by how many societies, in all forms, times, and places, even those proclaiming and implementing democratic principles, have difficulty in accepting the Other. The diaspora group, different, more or less visible, surviving by endogamy, often, in the event of a crisis, becomes a scapegoat. But here too we must not over-generalize. A less simplistic approach to the phenomenon of diasporas in history indicates changing and contradictory attitudes on the part of host states and populations.

For example, until the appearance of modern nationalism, Islam showed itself more tolerant than Christian countries toward the "People of the Book." Diasporas, perceived by states as nonterritorial minorities, have often in the past been the target of repression or assimilation. National socialism sought to annihilate the Jews and Gypsies. In a quite different context, the conditions which greeted racially different migrants, like the Chinese in democratic America, need no comment. Nevertheless, with time and contact, some groups do successfully live together and even integrate.

When discussing the itineraries and wanderings of populations scattered over time and space, it would be idle to expect a rigorous history consistently backed up by documents or statistics. The Gypsies are a good case in point. Often persecuted, diasporas are peoples or groups buffeted by history, living precariously and rarely having their chroniclers.[14] Yet perhaps we can affirm that the most dynamic diasporas of yesteryear[15] had as it were a headstart on the globalization of trade and communications that has occurred with the industrial age.

Gérard Chaliand and Jean-Pierre Rageau

14. Phillip D. Curtin, *Cross Cultural Trade in World History* (Cambridge: At the University Press, 1984).

15. See Fernand Braudel, *Capitalism and Material Life, 1400–1800,* trans. Miriam Kochan (London:Weidenfield, 1973).

▲ Synagogue of Curaçao, in the West Indies (Ph.© Douglas Dickins).

◄ Synagogue of Cochin, in India (Ph. © Robert Harding).

Old Synagogue of ► Prague (Ph. © Scala).

THE JEWISH DIASPORA

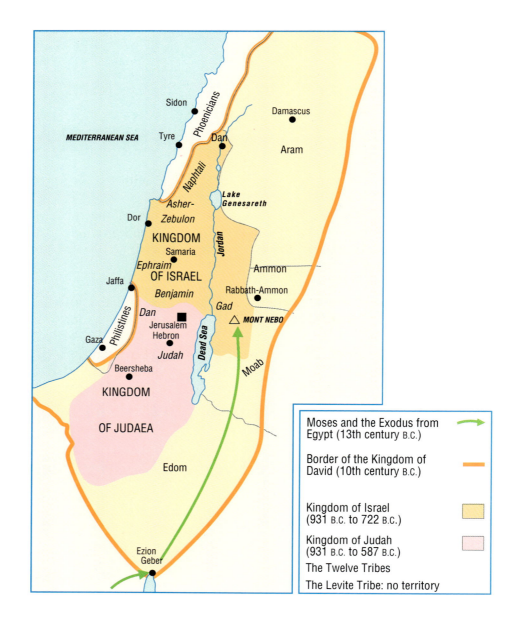

MEDITERRANEAN SEA

Sidon

Tyre

Phoenicians

Dan

Damascus

Aram

Naphtali

Lake
Genesareth

Asher-
Zebulon

Dor

KINGDOM

Samaria

Jordan

Ammon

Ephraim

OF ISRAEL

Jaffa

Benjamin

Rabbath-Ammon

Gad

Dan

△ *MONT NEBO*

Jerusalem

Hebron

Gaza

Philistines

Judah

Dead Sea

Moab

Beersheba

KINGDOM

OF JUDAEA

Edom

Ezion
Geber

Moses and the Exodus from
Egypt (13th century B.C.)

Border of the Kingdom of
David (10th century B.C.)

Kingdom of Israel
(931 B.C. to 722 B.C.)

Kingdom of Judah
(931 B.C. to 587 B.C.)

The Twelve Tribes

The Levite Tribe: no territory

Antiquity

The history of the Jewish people is inextricably linked with that of a religion.

If early antiquity ends, roughly, with the destruction of the Second Temple in A.D. 70, the date when Palestine became a Roman province and which marks the great dispersion, the history of the Jewish people can be divided into two periods.

The first runs from the thirteenth century B.C. to the Babylonian captivity following the taking of Jerusalem by the Chaldaean king Nebuchadnezzar (587 B.C.).

In that period, the ancestors of Israel, led by Moses, left Egypt and headed for the "promised land." The tribes that made up Israel gradually moved into the land of the Canaanites (thirteenth to eleventh centuries). Three rulers followed one another in the state created by the Jews: Saul (1030–1010); David, who made Jerusalem the capital; and Solomon, who ordered the building of the First Temple.

In 931 B.C. a split occurred and the northern tribes, centered in Samaria, kept the name of Israel, while the southern ones found themselves ruling the kingdom of Judah, with Jerusalem as its capital. In the ninth century religious literature and the first prophets appeared (Amos, Isaiah, etc.). A second generation of prophets appeared in the eighth century, while in 722 B.C. the northern kingdom collapsed: Samaria was destroyed by Sargon II, king

THE KINGDOM OF DAVID

of Assyria, leading to the deportation and dilution of the tribes. In 587 B.C. Nebuchadnezzar, the ruler of Chaldaea, conquered Jerusalem, destroyed the Temple, and deported part of the population to Babylon. Dispersion seems to be the hallmark of the Jewish people.

This first exile, 587–539 B.C., is the reference point for the various biblical texts (e.g., Ezekiel, Isaiah) that clearly delineate Judaism. In 539 B.C. Cyrus, king of Persia, conqueror of the Chaldaeans, allowed the exiles to return.

THE DESTRUCTION OF JERUSALEM

II Chronicles 36:14–17, 19–20.

Moreover all the chief of the priests, and the people, transgressed very much after all the abominations of the heathen; and polluted the house of the Lord which he had hallowed in Jerusalem. And the Lord God of their fathers sent to them by his messengers, rising up betimes, and sending; because he had compassion on his people, and on his dwelling place; But they mocked the messengers of God, and despised his words, and misused his prophets, until the wrath of the Lord arose against his people, till there was no remedy. Therefore he brought upon them the king of the Chaldees, who slew their young men with the sword in the house of their sanctuary, and had no compassion upon young man or maiden, old man, or him that stooped for age: he gave them all into his hand. . . . And they burnt the house of God, and brake down the wall of Jerusalem, and burnt all the palaces thereof with fire, and destroyed all the goodly vessels thereof. And them that had escaped from the sword carried he away to Babylon; where they were servants to him and his sons until the reign of the kingdom of Persia.[1]

1. All quotations from the Old Testament are from the English translation of the Hebrew Bible.

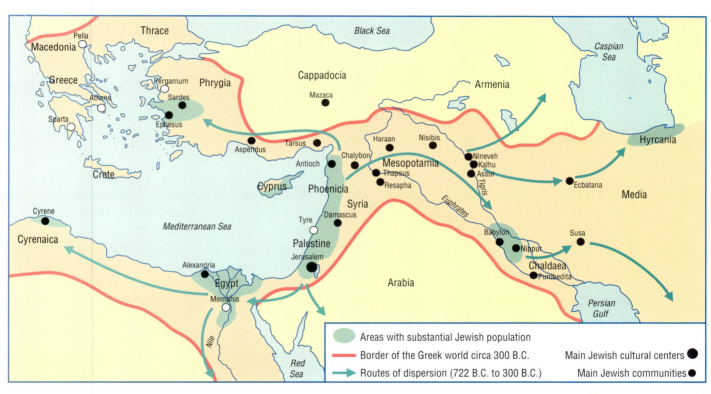

Areas with substantial Jewish population
Border of the Greek world circa 300 B.C.
Routes of dispersion (722 B.C. to 300 B.C.)
Main Jewish cultural centers ●
Main Jewish communities ●

THE FIRST DISPERSION ▲

THE HOPE OF RETURN
Isaiah 11:11–12.

And it shall come to pass in that day, that the Lord shall set his hand again the second time to recover the remnant of his people, which shall be left, from Assyria, and from Egypt, and from Pathros, and from Cush, and from Elam, and from Shinar, and from Hamath, and from the islands of the sea. And he shall set up an ensign for the nations, and shall assemble the outcasts of Israel, and gather together the dispersed of Judah from the four corners of the earth.

Ezekiel 37:12–14.

Therefore prophesy and say unto them, Thus saith the Lord God; Behold, O my people, I will open your graves, and cause you to come up out of your graves, and bring you into the land of Israel. And ye shall know that I am the Lord, when I have opened your graves, O my people, and brought you up out of your graves. And shall put my spirit in you, and ye shall live, and I shall place you in your own land: then shall ye know that I the Lord have spoken it, and performed it, saith the Lord.

END OF THE BABYLONIAN CAPTIVITY
Ezra 1:1–3.

Now in the first year of Cyrus, king of Persia, that the word of the Lord by the mouth of Jeremiah might be fulfilled, the Lord stirred up the spirit of Cyrus king of Persia, that he made a proclamation throughout all his kingdom, and put it also in writing, saying: Thus saith Cyrus king of Persia. The Lord God of heaven hath given me all the kingdoms of the earth; and he hath charged me to build him an house at Jerusalem, which is in Judah. Who is there among you of all his people? His God be with him, and let him go up to Jerusalem, which is in Judah, and build the house of the Lord God of Israel (he is the God), which is in Jerusalem.

The second period runs from the end of the exile (539 B.C.) to the capture of Jerusalem by the Romans and the destruction of the Second Temple (A.D. 70). Palestine then became a Roman province.

This period saw the defeat of the Persians by Alexander in the fourth century B.C. In the third and second centuries Palestine was dominated by the Ptolomies; Jewish colonies settled in the coastal cities of the eastern Mediterranean, especially Alexandria.

Thus in antiquity, Judaism had three great centers: Judaea, Babylon, and in the Hellenistic period, Alexandria. The philosopher Philo (first century) was the most illustrious among the Jews of Alexandria.

In the second century B.C., Jewish colonies settled in all the major centers of the Roman Empire, including Rome itself. In 63 B.C., Pompey took Jerusalem. The weight of Rome made itself felt, indirectly or directly, down to the fall of rebellious Jerusalem and the destruction of the Second Temple by Titus. Palestine became an integral part of the Roman Empire. The dispersion of the Jewish people this time was on a massive scale. Meanwhile, Christianity was beginning to spread.

The situation of the Jews in the Roman Empire—where at one time they enjoyed a charter granted by Julius Caesar dispensing them from any obligation that conflicted with their religion—was good until the first century A.D., when they were twice expelled, in 19 and 49. However, these measures did not last long and in A.D. 212 the Jews, like other groups, became citizens of the empire.

THE ROMAN EMPIRE

DESTRUCTION OF THE SECOND TEMPLE

Flavius Josephus, The Jewish War *(VI, 26–27), Grand Rapids Michigan, 1982, p. 421.*

Titus retired to the Antonia, intending to launch a full scale attack the following day at dawn and take possession of the Temple. The santuary, however, had long before been condemned by God to the flames; and now, after the passing of the years, the fated day was at hand, the tenth of the month of Lous—the very date when centuries before it had been burned by the king of Babylon.

CAESAR AND THE JEWS

Flavius Josephus, Antiquities of the Jews, *XIV, X, in E. Flegg,* The Jewish Anthology, *New York, 1940.*

The decree of Caesar: "I, Julius Caesar, imperator the second time, and High Priest, have made this decree with the approbation of the Senate: Whereas Hyrcanus, the son of Alexander the Jew, hath demonstrated his fidelity and diligence about our affairs, and this both now and in former times, both in peace and in war, as many of our generals have borne witness . . . For these reasons I will that Hyrcanus, the son of Alexander, and his children, be ethnarchs of the Jews and have the High Priesthood of the Jews for ever, and that he and his sons be our confederates; and that beside this every one of them be reckoned among our particular friends. I also ordain that he and his children retain whatever privileges belong to the office of High Priest, or whatsoever favors have hitherto been granted them; and if at any time hereafter there arise any questions about the Jewish customs, I will that he determine the same. And I think it not proper that they should be obliged to find us winter quarters, or that any money should be required of them."

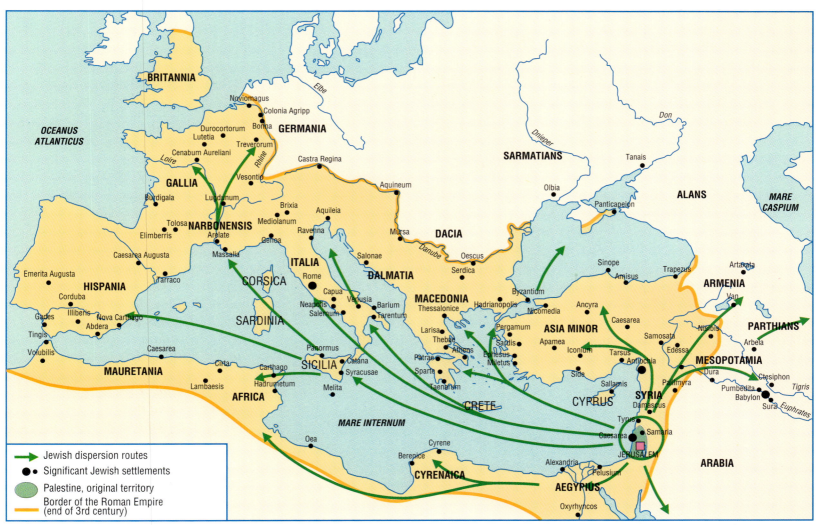

Jewish dispersion routes

● ● Significant Jewish settlements

Palestine, original territory

Border of the Roman Empire
(end of 3rd century)

JEWS IN THE ROMAN EMPIRE (C. A.D. 300) ▲

OCEANUS
ATLANTICUS

BRITANNIA

GERMANIA

Noviomagus
Colonia Agripp
Bonna
Durocortorum
Lutetia
Treverorum
Cenabum Aureliani
Vesontio

GALLIA

Burdigala
Lugdunum
NARBONENSIS
Tolosa
Arelate
Elimberris
Massalia

Castra Regina

Aquineum

SARMATIANS

Dnieper
Don

Tanais

Olbia

ALANS

MARE
CASPIUM

Panticapeion

HISPANIA

Caesarea Augusta
Tarraco
Corduba
Illiberis
Nova Carthago
Gades
Abdera
Tingis
Volubilis

Emerita Augusta

Brixia
Aquileia
Mediolanum
Genoa
Ravenna

CORSICA
ITALIA
Rome

Massalia

SARDINIA

Caesarea

MAURETANIA

Cirta
Carthago
Hadrumetum
Lambaesis

AFRICA

Salonae

DALMATIA

Mursa

DACIA

Oescus
Serdica

Danube

Byzantium

MACEDONIA
Thessalonice
Hadrianopolis
Nicomedia

Larisa
Thebae
Pergamum
Athens
Sardis
Patrae
Ephesus
Sparte
Miletus
Taenarum

Sinope
Amisus
Trapezus

ASIA MINOR
Ancyra
Caesarea

Apamea
Iconium
Tarsus

Side
Sallamis

Artaxata
Van

ARMENIA

PARTHIANS

Nisibis
Arbela
Samosata
Edessa

MESOPOTAMIA
Dura

SYRIA
Antiochia
Palmyra

Damascus

Ctesiphon
Pumbedita
Babylon
Sura

Tigris
Euphrates

Capua
Neapolis
Verusia
Salernum
Barium
Tarentum

Panormus
Catana
SICILIA
Syracusae
Melita

Oea

MARE INTERNUM

CRETE

CYPRUS

Tyrus
Caesarea
Samaria
JERUSALEM

ARABIA

Cyrene
Berenice

CYRENAICA

Alexandria
Pelusium

AEGYPTUS

Oxyrhyncos

B.C.

3760   Mythical date of the creation of the world. Year I of the Jewish era.

13th c.   Moses leads the Hebrews out of Egypt. Revelation of the Law on Mount Sinai.

13th–11th c.   The tribes of Israel move into the land of Canaan.

1030–1010   Saul, first king of Israel.

1010–970   Reign of David.

10th c.   Reign of Solomon (970–932). Building of the First Temple. Division of the kingdom (931): in the north, Israel, with its capital at Samaria; in the south, Judah, with its capital at Jerusalem.

9th c.   The first prophets.

8th–7th c.   Second generation of prophets.

722   Sargon II, king of Assyria, defeats the kingdom of Israel. Deportation and dispersion of the population.

587   Nebuchadnezzar, king of Chaldaea, puts an end to the kingdom of Judah and destroys the Temple of Jerusalem. Deportation of the population.

6th c.   The last prophets.

587–539   Babylonian Captivity. The Chaldaean Empire collapses. The Hebrews come under Persian rule. Cyrus II authorizes the rebuilding of the Temple.

333–332   Alexander the Great defeats the Persians and seizes Palestine.

320–198   Palestine under the rule of the Ptolomies. Jewish colonies settle in Damascus, Antioch, Ephesus, and, above all, Alexandria.

168–142   Antiochus IV, king of Syria, seeks to impose the Greek religion on the Jews. Revolt of the Maccabees.

ca. 150   Book of Daniel. Last of the prophetic texts of the Old Testament.

142   Palestine again becomes an independent state.

63   Pompey takes Jerusalem.

47   The diaspora Jews who have communities in all the major centers of the Roman Empire, and some of whom are citizens and electors in Rome, secure from Julius Caesar the right to send an annual tribute to the Temple (*fiscus judaicus*).

40   Herod, governor of Galilee, has himself named king of the Jews by the Roman senate.

4	Death of Herod. Revolt of the Jews.
A.D.	
26–36	Pontius Pilate is procurator of Judaea. Period of Jesus and the apostles. The Jews of Alexandria, seeing their interests threatened, send the great philosopher Philo (born in 30 B.C.) to Rome to ask exemption from the duty of worshiping the emperor.
50–60	Activity of Saint Paul (Saul of Tarsus). His travels. Christianity takes root in the Roman Empire outside Palestine.
64	Jewish revolt.
66	Vespasian sent by Rome to put an end to the revolt. The Jewish historian Flavius Josephus takes part in the revolt and then surrenders to the Romans.
70	Titus takes Jerusalem (destruction of the Second Temple) and takes many captives with him to Rome, including Flavius Josephus. Palestine becomes a Roman province. New dispersion into Arabia, Georgia, Crimea, Italy, Gaul, Spain.

As far back as Antiquity, the Torah (the biblical books of the Pentateuch) ▶ has denoted the Law. From the first century on, the "oral Torah" has included all the rabbinic lessons as well. Maimonides's *Mishne Torah* (The Repetition of the Law), shown here in an 1180 manuscript, codifies the whole talmudic law. (National and University Library of Jerusalem. Photo © Giraudon.)

BABYLON When the Roman Empire became Christian in the fourth century, the situation changed and there was great religious intolerance. The center of Judaism had already shifted from Palestine to Babylon.

In the third century A.D. a religious academy was founded in Babylon, where the diaspora had been large and active since the Captivity. At about the same time, another academy was created at Pumbedita (Mesopotamia).

It was also in Babylon that the most important version of the Talmud (tradition), called the Babli (sixth century), was composed, while another version was compiled at Jerusalem (the Jerushalmi). The two great academies at Sura and Pumbedita were the major centers of Judaic thought from the fifth and sixth to the ninth centuries.

Generally, the Jews in the East enjoyed relative autonomy. This was the case in Babylon under the Assyro-Chaldaeans, the Persians, the Parthians, and later the Muslims.

Jews in the Christian world (c. 600) ▶

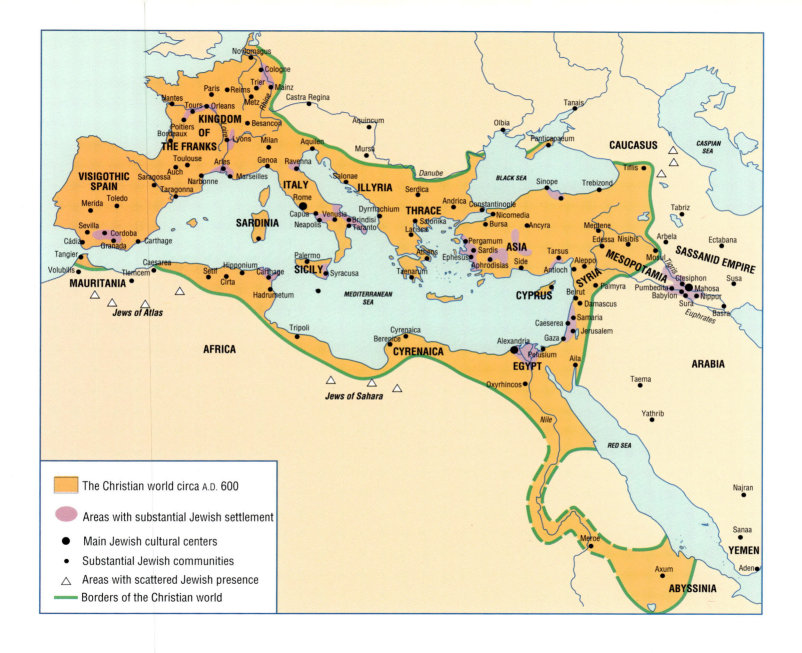

Novomagus
Cologne
Trier
Paris Reims Mainz
Nantes Metz Castra Regina
Tours Orleans
KINGDOM Besançon Aquincum
Poitiers OF Lyons Mursa Olbia Panticapaeum CAUCASUS CASPIAN SEA
Bordeaux THE FRANKS Milan Aquilen
Toulouse Genoa Ravenna Danube Tanais Tiflis
Arles Salonae BLACK SEA
Auch Marseilles ITALY ILLYRIA Serdica Sinope Trebizond
Saragossa Narbonne Rome Andrica Constantinople
VISIGOTHIC Taragonna Capua Venusia THRACE Nicomedia Tabriz
SPAIN Neapolis Brindisi Salonika Bursa Ancyra Meptene
Merida Toledo Taranto Latissa Edessa Nisibis Arbela Ectabana
SARDINIA Pergamum Sardis ASIA Tarsus Aleppo MESOPOTAMIA
Sevilla Dyrrhachium Aphrodisias Side Antioch SYRIA Ctesiphon
Cordoba Athens Ephesus SASSANID EMPIRE
Cádiz Carthage Taenarum CYPRUS Belrut Palmyra Susa
Granada Damascus Pumbedita Mahosa
Tangier Caesarea Palermo SICILY Babylon Nippur
Volubilis Tlemcem Hipponium Syracusa Caeserea Samaria Sura Basra
MAURITANIA Setif Carthage Gaza Jerusalem Euphrates
Cirta MEDITERRANEAN Alexandria
Hadrumetum SEA Pelusium Aila
Tripoli Cyrenaica ARABIA
Berenice Oxyrhincos Taema
AFRICA CYRENAICA EGYPT
Jews of Sahara Yathrib
Jews of Atlas Nile
RED SEA
Najran
Meroe
Sanaa
Axum YEMEN
ABYSSINIA Aden

The Christian world circa A.D. 600

Areas with substantial Jewish settlement

● Main Jewish cultural centers

• Substantial Jewish communities

△ Areas with scattered Jewish presence

━━ Borders of the Christian world

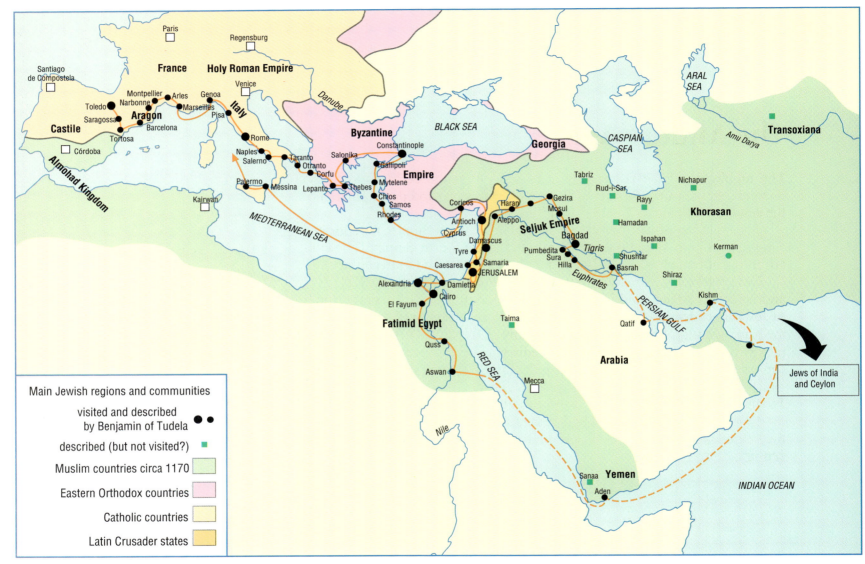

▲ The journey of Benjamin of Tudela

Paris
Regensburg
Santiago de Compostela
France
Holy Roman Empire
Montpellier
Arles
Genoa
Venice
Narbonne
Marseilles
Toledo
Aragon
Pisa
Italy
Saragossa
Barcelona
Castile
Tortosa
Rome
Córdoba
Almohad Kingdom
Naples
Salerno
Taranto
Salonika
Constantinople
Byzantine
BLACK SEA
Georgia
ARAL SEA
Amu Darya
Transoxiana
Otranto
Corfu
Gallipoli
Empire
Kairwan
Palermo
Messina
Lepanto
Thebes
Mytelene
Chios
Samos
Rhodes
Coricos
Haran
Gezira
Mosul
Tabriz
Rud-i-Sar
Rayy
Nichapur
Khorasan
MEDITERRANEAN SEA
Antioch
Aleppo
Seljuk Empire
Hamadan
Cyprus
Damascus
Bagdad
Tigris
Ispahan
Kerman
Tyre
Pumbedita
Sura
Shushtar
Caesarea
Samaria
Hilla
Basrah
Shiraz
Alexandria
Damietta
JERUSALEM
Euphrates
Kishm
Cairo
PERSIAN GULF
El Fayum
Fatimid Egypt
Taima
Qatif
Quss
RED SEA
Arabia
Jews of India and Ceylon
Aswan
Mecca
Nile
Taima
Sanaa
Yemen
Aden
INDIAN OCEAN
CASPIAN SEA
Danube

The Middle Ages

The highlights of the fifteen centuries separating the destruction of the Second Temple (A.D. 70, start of the great dispersion) and the expulsion of the Jews from Spain in 1492 are as follows.

The situation of the Jewish diaspora in the Roman Empire deteriorated when Christianity became the state religion in the fourth century. The situation was not much better at Byzantium under Justinian (sixth century).

Conversely, Muslim rule improved the condition of the Jews in Alexandria, North Africa, and in Spain. Babylon continued as the great center of Jewish academies (yeshivas at Sura and Pumbedita) until the middle of the ninth century. Spain, with the Academy at Córdoba (950), became the most prosperous Jewish center in the Mediterranean in the tenth and eleventh centuries. The situation deteriorated under the Almohads, ca. 1150; Portugal welcomed the Jews. In medieval western Europe, on the other hand, anti-Judaism emerged and the Jews were expelled from many countries. From the fourteenth century they found refuge in Poland and Lithuania, where they enjoyed a favorable status and prerogatives until the mid-seventeenth century.

◀ THE JOURNEY OF BENJAMIN OF TUDELA.

In the mid-twelfth century, while the rule of the Almohads in Spain was marked by religious intolerance, Rabbi Benjamin of Tudela undertook a journey from 1160 to 1173 to survey the communities in the diaspora.

This journey took him from Spain to the Middle East, by way of Constantinople. He visited most of the Jewish communities and described those in Iran and India from the reports of eyewitnesses that he met—thereby missing only that of Kaifeng, in China, where a colony from Persia had settled in the eleventh century.

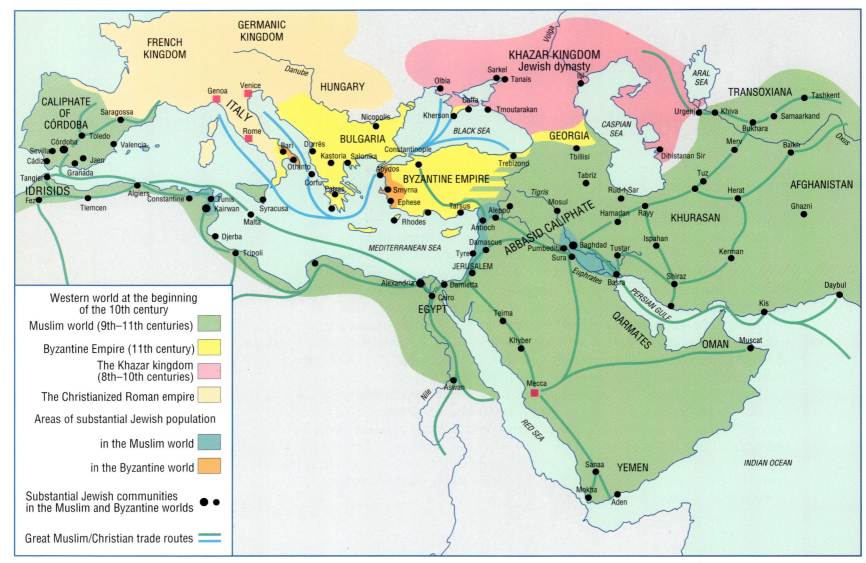

▲ JEWS IN THE MUSLIM AND BYZANTINE WORLD (c. A.D. 900)

Map labels

FRENCH KINGDOM

GERMANIC KINGDOM

KHAZAR KINGDOM
Jewish dynasty

TRANSOXIANA

ARAL SEA

Volga

Danube

HUNGARY

Sarkel

Tanais

Tashkent

CALIPHATE OF CÓRDOBA

Saragossa

ITALY

Genoa

Venice

Olbia

Caffa

Urgenj

Khiva

Samaarkand

Córdoba

Toledo

Rome

Nicopolis

Kherson

Tmoutarakan

BLACK SEA

CASPIAN SEA

GEORGIA

Dihistanan Sir

Bukhara

Balkh

Oxus

Sevilla

Cádiz

Valencia

Bari

Durrës

BULGARIA

Constantinople

Trebizond

Tbillisi

Tabriz

Merv

Tuz

Jaen

Granada

Otranto

Kastoria

Salonika

Abydos

Rud-i Sar

Rayy

KHURASAN

Herat

AFGHANISTAN

Tangier

IDRISIDS

Fez

Algiers

Constantine

Corfu

Patras

BYZANTINE EMPIRE

Smyrna

Ephese

Tarsus

Aleppo

Tigris

Mosul

Hamadan

ABBASID CALIPHATE

Ispahan

Ghazni

Tlemcen

Tunis

Kairwan

Syracusa

Rhodes

Antioch

Damascus

Pumbedita

Baghdad

Tustar

Kerman

Malta

Djerba

Tripoli

MEDITERRANEAN SEA

Tyre

JERUSALEM

Sura

Euphrates

Basra

Shiraz

PERSIAN GULF

Daybul

Alexandria

Damietta

Cairo

EGYPT

Teima

Khyber

Nile

Aswan

Mecca

RED SEA

Kis

QARMATES

OMAN

Muscat

INDIAN OCEAN

Sanaa

YEMEN

Mokha

Aden

Legend

Western world at the beginning of the 10th century

Muslim world (9th–11th centuries)

Byzantine Empire (11th century)

The Khazar kingdom (8th–10th centuries)

The Christianized Roman empire

Areas of substantial Jewish population

in the Muslim world

in the Byzantine world

Substantial Jewish communities in the Muslim and Byzantine worlds

Great Muslim/Christian trade routes

The lightning expansion of Islam in the seventh and eighth centuries brought a very significant proportion of the Jewish people, from the Middle East to Spain, under Muslim rule. Islam has always been tolerant toward the People of the Book. They retained their religious autonomy and, as long as they paid tribute, saw to the affairs of their communities.

ISLAM

In contrast to Byzantium and the Christian West, the Jews enjoyed a period of prosperity and peace under Muslim rule, from the eighth to the mid-twelfth centuries, notably in Spain, at Toledo, Córdoba, and Granada. The situation of the Jews in Spain reached its height in the tenth and eleventh centuries when Hasadai Ibn Shaprut was doctor and adviser to the sultan of Córdoba and Samuel ibn Nagdela (ca. 993–1060) became the vizier of the ruler of Granada.

At the time when the role of Babylon was declining, Spain (the Academy of Córdoba was established in 950) and North Africa (Kairwan) took over. A small surviving Jewish community at Tiberias in Palestine played an important role spiritually.

In the tenth century Egypt was conquered by the Fatimids, who proved to be tolerant in the early years of the dynasty. The kingdom's first vizier was a Jew from Baghdad, Jacob ibn Killis (who converted to Islam). When the Fatimid dynasty came to an end in 1168 Egypt came under the rule of the Kurd Saladin. His doctor was Maimonides (1135–1204), whose family had left Spain not long before. Maimonides's writings aroused considerable controversies among learned Jews.

THE WEST   In the eleventh and twelfth centuries, in a climate marked by Crusades and reconquest (Toledo was retaken in 1085), an anti-semitism developed that culminated in massacres in western Europe. In 1245 the Lateran Council provided a legal basis for this rejection and the Jews were henceforth required to wear a skullcap as a distinguishing mark.

Numerous Jewish religious academies (yeshivas) were closed and the Jews were banished from the kingdoms of England and France.

In 1290 Edward I of England, with the support of the Church, expelled the Jews and confiscated their property. The Jews did not return to England until the seventeenth century. Those expelled moved to northern France and to Germany.

Between 1132 and 1321 the Jews in the kingdom of France were expelled and recalled four times. Philip the Fair in particular expelled them in 1306. A final expulsion in 1394 remained in force in many provinces of France until the Revolution.

There were no restrictions on the professional or economic activities of Jews in Rome, Byzantium, or the Muslim countries. But there were in the medieval West. The Jews could not own land, or become members of a guild of Christian traders or craftsmen. After the First Crusade, in the eleventh century, the Jews in the West, when they could, became moneylenders, with an international commercial network.

From the fourteenth century Jews persecuted by the Christians in western Europe found refuge in the kingdom of Poland. Rulers such as Casimir III the Great (1333–1370) granted them all sorts of rights, and until the seventeenth century the Jews in Poland, as in neighboring Lithuania, were safe. Most came from Germany, and Yiddish became the language of the Ashkenazim (Germans). Numerous yeshivas were opened in Poland and Lithuania. Further east, Jewish colonies continued to survive from ancient times in the Crimea, around the Black Sea, in Ukraine, and in Bessarabia.

In the twelfth and thirteenth centuries the active centers around the Mediterranean were Alexandria; Kairwan; Fez; Spain; Palermo, especially under Roger II (1112–1154) and Frederick II (1198–1250); Montpellier, Avignon, and Orange in Provence; and Pisa, Lucca, and Rome in Italy.

In the Muslim world too the thirteenth and fourteenth centuries were a period in which the Jews suffered persecution, in both Egypt and Spain.

The Jews played an important role as mediators between the culture of Muslim Spain and the Christian culture of western Europe.

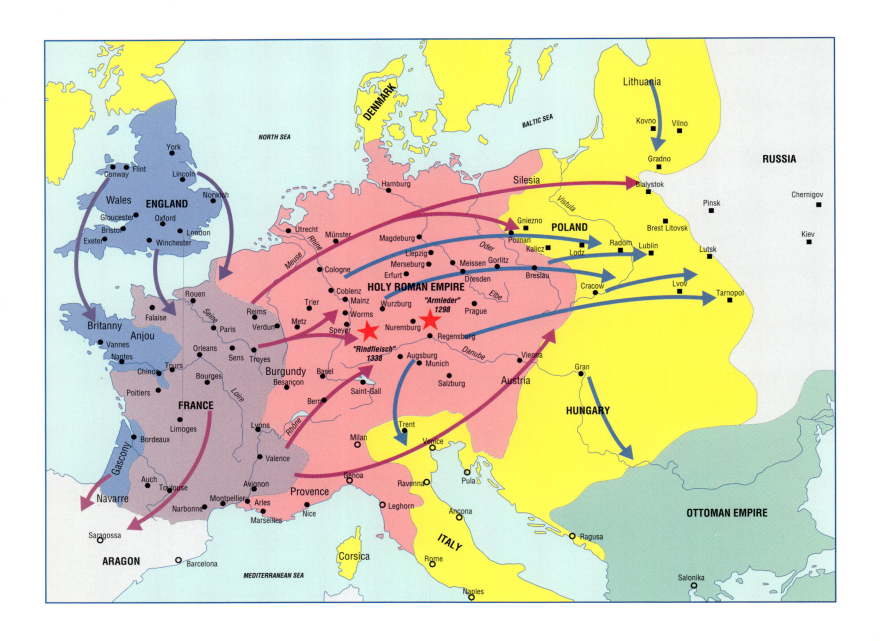

Regions forbidden to Jews

before 1300 ■

before 1400 ■

Prohibitions varying according
to place and time before 1500 ■

Other Catholic countries ■

Muslim world circa 1500 ■

Migration

from England in the 8th century ⟶

from France (14th–15th centuries) ⟶

from the Holy Roman Empire
(14th–15th centuries) ⟶

Guest communities and centers
of new Jewish settlement ■

Major Jewish communities in
Western Europe ●

Other significant
Jewish communities ○

Slaughter of Jews
by the "Armleder",
Central Germany (1298–1303) ★

Slaughter of Jews
by "Rindfleisch" in
Franconia and Alsace (1336–1338) ★

133–136	Rebellion of Bar Kochba in Palestine crushed.
211–217	Reign of Caracalla. All Jews in the empire have access to Roman magistracies.
220	Under Parthian rule, the Jews of Babylon are governed by an exilarch. Founding of the Academy of Sura.
306–337	Reign of Constantine, first Christian emperor.
4th c.	Compilation of the Jerusalem Talmud being completed.
395	Division between the Western and Eastern Roman Empires.
418	The Jews in the Western Empire excluded from all public offices.
411–484	Spain is conquered by the Visigoths, who profess Arianism (a Christian heresy). They leave the Jews full religious freedom.
476	Fall of Rome signals final dissolution of Western Empire.
6th c.	Completion of the compilation of the Babylonian Talmud.
511	Under Sassanid rule, the Jews enjoy a great measure of autonomy in Babylon under the exilarch Mar Zutra II.
537	Edict of the emperor Justinian depriving the Jews of civil equality and religious freedom.

◄ THE FLIGHT OF JEWS FROM THE MEDIEVAL WEST

612	After the Visigothic kings have converted from Arianism and submitted to the authority of the Church, the Jews in Spain are forced to choose between exile and baptism.
629	Dagobert, king of the Franks, warns Jews to choose between baptism and exile.
637	The Muslims take Jerusalem.
651	The Jews of Babylon come under Muslim rule.
711	Muslim conquest of Spain. The Jews gain their religious freedom.
8th c.	The Khazars (southern Russia) convert to Judaism.
950	Founding of the yeshiva (academy) of Córdoba. The Jews enjoy religious autonomy and some occupy very high posts under Abd el Rahman, sultan of Córdoba.
11th–12th c.	Founding of the yeshiva of Mainz, and those of Troyes and Narbonne.
1096	First Crusade, accompanied by many massacres of Jews in Germany and France.
1144	First accusation of ritual murder (England).
1146	Second Crusade. Massacres of Jews in France.
1148	Persecutions of Jews by the Almohads in Spain.
1181	Philip Augustus orders Paris yeshiva closed.

1254	Saint Louis banishes the Jews from France.
1274	In a bull Pope Gregory X denies the existence of ritual murders.
1290	Expulsion of the Jews from England.
1321	In France, the Jews are accused, along with the lepers, of a plot to poison wells for the Muslims of Granada.
1334	Casimir III of Poland grants the Jews the *Privilegium Fredericanum*
1348–1349	The Black Death is blamed on the Jews. Tens of thousands of them are burned in western Europe.
1391	Massacre of Jews in Castile and Aragon.
1481–1482	Inquisition established in Castile and Aragon, directed against the Marranos.*
1492	Expulsion of the Jews from Spain. Among places of welcome are the Ottoman Empire, Morocco, and soon after, the Netherlands, once it is freed from Spanish rule.

Marranos: Jews in the Iberian peninsula, converted to Christianity against their will, some of whom practiced Judaism in secret. In the seventeenth century there were many Marranos in the Netherlands, where they returned to their original faith. They also formed the Jewish diaspora in the New World.

I questioned the ambassadors touching the fate of our Jewish brothers scattered throughout the exile, asking them if they had heard anything concerning those of them who languished in eternal slavery; but none could satisfy me, until the messengers from Khorazan, merchants, brought me reports of a state belonging to the Jews, the land of the Khazars. Then I humbled myself, adoring the God of heaven, and I sought around me a faithful messenger, to send him to your country that I might learn the whole truth regarding the happy condition of the king my master as well as his subjects, our brothers. . . . I therefore ask Your Majesty to bethink him of the eager desires of his servant, and notwithstanding the great distance to command his private scribes to send an affirmative answer to his servant, that I might know all concerning their condition, and that I might learn how Judaism was brought into your country. . . .

THE KINGDOM OF THE KHAZARS

Letter from Hasdai Ibn Shaprut, doctor and adviser to the sultan of Córdoba, to the king of the Khazars (ca. 958). The Khazars were a people in southern Russia who had embraced Judaism in the eighth century. From Carmoly, Travels in the Holy Land, *in E. Flegg,* The Jewish Anthology *(New York, 1940).*

THE FIRST CRUSADE

Joseph Ha-Cohen, The Vale of Tears, *in E. Flegg,* The Jewish Anthology *(New York, 1940)*

In the reign of Philip, son of Henry, King of France, Peter the Hermit went to Jerusalem, saw the sufferings of the Christians who lived there and, on his return, related it to his brothers; this was in the year 4856, which is the year 1096. The Christian kings then offered to go and conquer Judah and Jerusalem; from all countries there gathered an enormous concourse of men and women who would go with them, and with this year began a time of pitiless desolation for the Israelites in Christian countries, wherever they were scattered: and the times were such that they became sick of life; terrible and numberless were the inflictions they bore, for there rose against them the multitude of France and Germany which had gathered for the Crusade, an evil-faced multitude, which neither spared the aged nor took pity on children. Their cry was: "Let us avenge our Saviour on the Jews, let us wipe them out from among the peoples, unless they accept another god and become Christians like ourselves; and only when this is accomplished will we set out. . . . The Crusaders descended like night wolves against the holy community of Worms, and many of the members took refuge in the house of the Bishop, for fear of disaster. The attackers rushed into the houses and put to the sword whomsoever they found, sparing neither man nor woman. . . . As to the slaughtered, they sanctified the Holy One of Israel in the open light, and chose death rather than life that they might not become faithless to God. Many immolated themselves, and this one slew his brother, or his friend, his beloved wife, his sons and daughters: tender mothers slaughtered with firm hand their little children, and the little ones pronounced the Unity of God as they gave up their souls on the bosoms of their mothers.

. . .

In the time of the just king Alfonso the Old [fourteenth century], someone came and told the magistrates of the country that, on Easter eve, a Christian had entered the house of a Jew, cries for help had been heard and he had not been seen since. A search was at once made of the Jew's house, but nothing was found. The king did not believe in the crime. "That Jew," he said, "is an old man, he doesn't even have the strength to kill a fly." But the accusers stuck to what they had said and brought false witnesses who even gave the name of the Christian who had been killed. They said, "It was one Pedro Guzman, the husband of Beatrix, the vicar's house-keeper"; and they gave a detailed description of him. The Jew was put to the torture; he confessed and was condemned to be burnt. Just as the sentence was being proclaimed through the town, the bishop happened to pass by on his way to see the king. "What is this I am hearing?" he asked. "According to the sentence Pedro Guzman was killed by the Jew on 1 January, and just yesterday I saw that very Guzman in a village near the town; he will be here today or tomorrow." "Why then," asked the king, "did the Jew confess?" "Words extracted by torture," replied the bishop, "are just as deceptive as the actions of lords."

By the fear of heaven and by the glory of God, I bear witness that the number of the children of Israel who were in Spain was three hundred thousand, in the year in which their splendor was despoiled; and the value of their belongings, in houses and in furnishings, and the abundance of their blessings was more than ten million gold ducats, a wealth which they had accumulated against the day of misfortune. And today, four years after the expulsion, everything has disappeared.

THE ACCUSATION OF RITUAL MURDER

Text by Salomon Ibn Verga (late fifteenth-early sixteenth c.). A witness to the persecutions of the Jews in Portugal and Spain, he was spared as a Marrano but took refuge in the Ottoman Empire, where he returned to the religion of his forefathers and wrote his Schebet Jehuda *(Scourge of the Jews), the story of the persecutions sufffered by the Jews (Source: Isidore Loeb,* Revue des Etudes juives, *Paris).*

EXILE FROM SPAIN

Isaac Abrabanel (1437–1508), adviser to Alfonso V of Portugal; preface to the Commentary on Daniel, *in E. Flegg,* The Jewish Anthology *(New York, 1940).*

KINGDOM OF FRANCE

KINGDOM OF NAVARRA

La Coruña
Santiago de Compostela
Astorga
Leon
Sahagún
Burgos
Valmaseda
Vitoria
Pampelona
Perpignan
Orense
Tudela
Huesca
Figueras
Chaves
Soria
Saragossa
Lárida
Gerona
Barcelos
Valladolid
Douro
Osma
Catalayud
KINGDOM
Barcelona
Bragança
Zamora
Ebro
Porto
Medina del Campo
Segovia
OF ARAGON
Tarragona
Viseu
Guadalajara
Salamanca
Ávila
Coimbra
Rodrigo
Béjar
Madrid
TerueL
Tortosa
Guarda
Talavera de la Reina
Tagus
Cuenca
Tomar
Alcántara
Toledo
Santarém
Caceres
Guadalupe
Valencia
Lisbon
Mérida
Evora
Ciudad Real
Denia
Setúbal
Badajoz
Campo di Montiel
Beja
Llerena
Almagro
Alicante
Guadiana
Villanueva
Murcia
Elche
Córdoba
Guadalquivir
Sevilla
Jaén
Lorca
Cartagena
Castro Marim
Lucena
Granada
Faro
Écija
Cádiz
Málaga
KINGDOM OF GRANADA

KINGDOM OF CASTILE AND LEON

KINGDOM OF PORTUGAL

KINGDOM OF MAJORCA (ARAGON)
Palma
Arta

Tangier
Ceuta
Melilla

Legend:

Important Jewish communities ●
● (small)

Under Spanish control circa 1050

Spanish Reconquista (11th–12th centuries)

Spanish Reconquista (13th–14th centuries)

Muslim Kingdom of Granada (circa 1480)

Borders of 1475

▲ Jews on the Iberian peninsula during the Middle Ages

The Sephardim

In 1492 the Jews were expelled from Spain. Part of the community moved to Portugal and finally ended up in northern Europe, but most took refuge in countries around the Mediterranean: particularly in Morocco and Tunisia (where the Jewish community of Kairwan dates back to the eighth century), Italy, and Egypt. Many of them were welcomed in a rapidly expanding Ottoman Empire. A handful of Jews went to Safed in upper Galilee where a small Jewish community existed. Safed was, with Jerusalem, Hebron, and Tiberias, one of the four holy cities of Judaism.

Among the Maghreb countries, Morocco always occupied a special place. The Jewish diaspora in Morocco—Fez, Marrakech—long exercised an influence on that of the Jews in Spain and it prospered from the trans-Saharan trade. The sultan of Morocco welcomed the Jews after 1492. It was Jews from Morocco who from the sixteenth century began to settle in the Azores, at Madeira, and in the Canaries. Some of the Jews from the Balearic Islands and Catalonia took refuge in Algeria.

The sixteenth century was an especially prosperous century for the Jews in the Ottoman Empire. They secured important positions in economic life. For two decades (1553–1574) Joseph Nasi held leading diplomatic and financial positions in the service of the sultan.

The Jewish population in the Iberian peninsula

	Jews	Total pop.
SPAIN		
ca. 1250	150,000	5,500,000
ca. 1490	250,000	6,500,000
PORTUGAL		
ca. 1250	40,000	1,000,000
ca. 1490	80,000	1,200,000

THE OTTOMAN EMPIRE

The decline of the Ottoman Empire's commercial prosperity in the seventeenth century brought with it a corresponding decline of the Jews. Sabbatai Zevi proclaimed himself the messiah in 1648 and the emotion that this event aroused throughout the diaspora, well beyond the Ottoman Empire, made the political loyalty of the Jewish community suspect in the eyes of the sultan. Threatened with death, Sabbatai Zevi became a Muslim. The *dönmeh*[1] date from this time. Greeks and Armenians held the most important positions from the second half of the seventeenth century.

Under the Ottomans and under Muslim rule in general, Jews, like other religious minorities, were excluded from certain activities—such as soldiering—and occupied a status below that of Muslims. They were obliged to wear a yellow turban. But their religious autonomy was respected and they could occupy high office.

The Ottoman conquest in 1517 improved the status of the Jews in Egypt, where they had experienced a prolonged period of intolerance. Like Damascus, conquered by the Ottomans in 1516, Alexandria and Cairo were thriving centers for the Sephardic communities of the empire.[2]

The Sephardim, originally from Spain, spoke Ladino (Judaeo-Spanish), which is sixteenth-century Spanish. This language is spoken today by Sephardic communities in Bulgaria, Greece, and Turkey.[3]

The city of Salonika became one in which the Jews played a considerable role. In the seventeenth century the Sephardim of Constantinople and Salonika were important links in international trade between the Mediterranean, Amsterdam, and the East.

1. Converts. At the beginning of the twentieth century, there would be many *dönmeh* among the Young Turks in Salonika who were preparing the 1908 revolution.

2. The Sephardim are derived from the dispersion created by the expulsion of the Jews from Spain and the Iberian peninsula in 1492. These Judaeo-Spaniards spread all over the Mediterranean basin (Ottoman Empire, Italy, etc.). Some moved to northern Europe (Holland) and others founded the first Jewish communities in America.

Today they number 3.5 to 4 million and most live in Israel.

3. These Ladino speakers are distinct from the Arabic-speaking Jews of Iraq and Egypt.

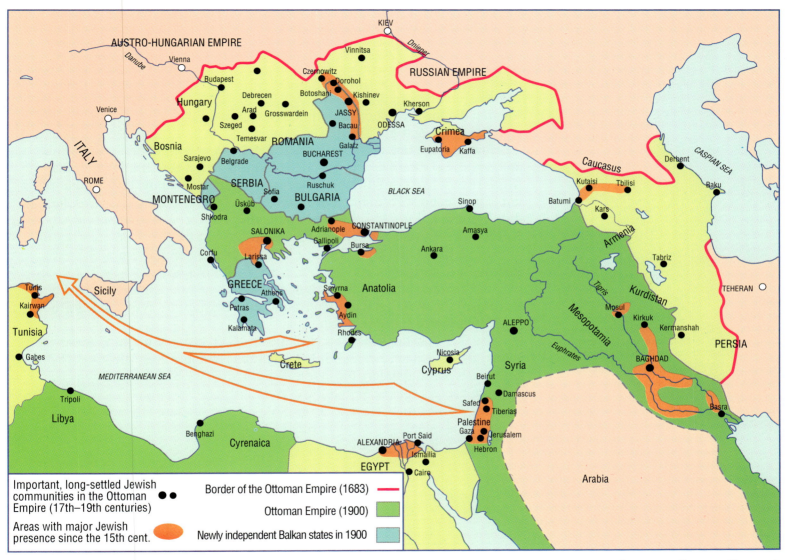

AUSTRO-HUNGARIAN EMPIRE

Danube
Vienna
Budapest
Hungary
Debrecen
Arad   Grosswardein
Szeged
Temesvar
Bosnia   ROMANIA
Sarajevo   Belgrade
Venice
Mostar   SERBIA
ROME   MONTENEGRO   Sofia
Üsküb
Shkodra
SALONIKA
Corfu   Larissa
Sicily   GREECE   Athens
Patras
Kalamata

Vinnitsa
RUSSIAN EMPIRE
Czernowitz
Dorohol
Botoshani
Debrecen   Kishinev
Kherson
JASSY   ODESSA
Bacau
Galatz
BUCHAREST
Ruschuk
BULGARIA   BLACK SEA
Adrianople   CONSTANTINOPLE
Gallipoli   Bursa
Smyrna
Aydin
Rhodes

Dnieper
KIEV

Crimea
Eupatoria   Kaffa

Caucasus
Kutaisi   Tbilisi   CASPIAN SEA
Batumi   Derbent
Kars   Baku
Sinop   Armenia
Amasya   Tabriz
Ankara   Kurdistan
Anatolia   Mosul   Kirkuk   TEHERAN
Kermanshah
Mesopotamia   PERSIA
ALEPPO   BAGHDAD
Nicosia   Syria   Euphrates
Cyprus   Beirut   Basra
Tigris
Damascus
Safed   Tiberias
Palestine
Gaza   Jerusalem
Hebron

ITALY

Tunis
Kairwan
Tunisia
Gabes

MEDITERRANEAN SEA   Crete

Tripoli
Libya   Benghazi   Cyrenaica

Port Said
ALEXANDRIA
Ismailia
EGYPT   Caire

Arabia

Important, long-settled Jewish
communities in the Ottoman
Empire (17th–19th centuries)

Areas with major Jewish
presence since the 15th cent.

Border of the Ottoman Empire (1683)

Ottoman Empire (1900)

Newly independent Balkan states in 1900

JEWS IN THE OTTOMAN EMPIRE ▲

ITALY

Some of the Jews expelled from Spain went to Italy, where very ancient communities still existed.

However, the centers of the colonies in Sicily and the south of the peninsula—Naples, Amalfi, Bari, Brindisi, Taranto—after thriving in the Middle Ages, ceased to exist with the Spanish occupation in the sixteenth century. But Rome, expecially in the time of the Medici popes—Leo X (1513–1521) and Clement VII (1523–1534)—remained sympathetic toward the Jews.

Jewish communities thrived in central Italy in the sixteenth century in Urbino, Ferrara, Florence, Spoleto, Siena, Ancona, and above all Mantua, then the second Jewish community in Italy after Venice.

The Venice *ghetto*[1] was instituted in 1516; it was perceived as an improvement, as the Jews had hitherto not had the right to live in the city but had been required to live at Giudecca.

Leghorn—which became a free port in 1675—played an important role in the history of the Jews in Italy through the close links it maintained with the Jewish communities of Smyrna, Salonika, Tunis, and Tripoli.

1. The *ghetto nuovo* or new foundry was allocated to the Ashkenazim; the *ghetto vecchio* (old ghetto) to Jews from the eastern Mediterranean. The Rome ghetto dates from 1555.

The dispersion of the Jews of the Iberian peninsula

Expelled: 160,000
to the Ottoman Empire 90,000
to the Netherlands 25,000
to Morocco 20,000   Casualties: 20,000
to France 10,000   Converts: 50,000
to Italy 10,000
to America 5,000?

THE DISPERSION OF THE SEPHARDIM ▶
Spain drove the Jews out in 1492. Naples became Spanish in 1504; the expulsions in southern Italy began only at that time. Expelled to America, the Jews settled in Dutch Brazil (Pernambuco, Ceará, Bahai). In 1654 Brazil came under Portuguese rule and the Jews had to emigrate to the Dutch West Indies (Curaçao) and North America (Newport).

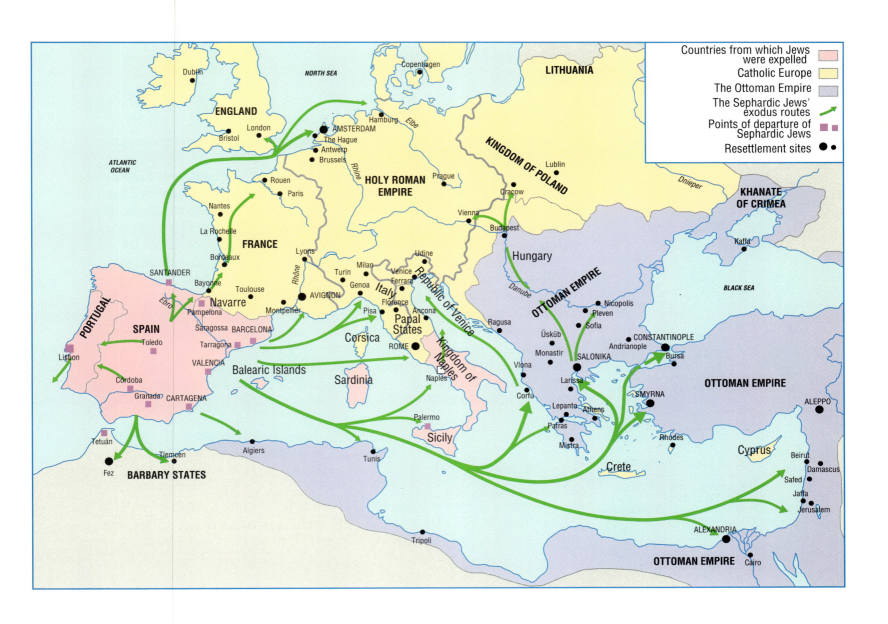

Legend:
- Countries from which Jews were expelled
- Catholic Europe
- The Ottoman Empire
- The Sephardic Jews' exodus routes
- Points of departure of Sephardic Jews
- Resettlement sites

DUBLIN

ENGLAND

NORTH SEA

Copenhagen

LITHUANIA

London
Bristol

ATLANTIC OCEAN

Hamburg
Elbe

AMSTERDAM
The Hague
Antwerp
Brussels

Rouen

Paris

Nantes

La Rochelle

FRANCE

Bordeaux

Bayonne

SANTANDER

Navarre

Pampelona

PORTUGAL

Ebro

SPAIN

Toledo

Saragossa   BARCELONA

Tarragona

Lisbon

Cordoba

Granada

CARTAGENA

VALENCIA

Tetuán

Fez

Tlemcen

BARBARY STATES

Toulouse

Montpelier

AVIGNON

Lyons

Rhône

Turin   Milan

Genoa

Italy

Pisa

Florence

Papal
States

ROME

Corsica

Sardinia

Balearic Islands

Algiers

Tunis

Tripoli

HOLY ROMAN
EMPIRE

Rhine

Prague

KINGDOM OF POLAND

Lublin

Cracow

Vienna

Budapest

Danube

Hungary

OTTOMAN EMPIRE

Udine

Venice
Ferrara

Republic of Venice

Ancona

Kingdom of
Naples

Naples

Palermo

Sicily

Ragusa

Vlona

Corfu

Lepanto

Patras

Mistra

Nicopolis
Pleven

Sofia

Üsküb

Monastir

SALONIKA

Larissa

Athens

Dnieper

KHANATE
OF CRIMEA

Kaffa

CONSTANTINOPLE
Andrianople

Bursa

SMYRNA

Rhodes

BLACK SEA

OTTOMAN EMPIRE

Cyprus

Crete

ALEPPO

Beirut
Damascus

Safed

Jaffa

Jerusalem

ALEXANDRIA

Cairo

OTTOMAN EMPIRE

THE NETHERLANDS

After the great period of prosperity and cultural flowering of Muslim Spain, it was in the Netherlands that the Jews flourished in the seventeenth century.

Large numbers of Jews, especially Marranos, moved from Spain and Portugal to the Netherlands. By the beginning of the seventeenth century they were firmly established in Holland and returned to the cult that they had had to abandon. In 1615 the Dutch authorities left it up to each province to decide whether or not it wished to admit Jews. Some did, others did not. Although there were economic and social restrictions (they were banned from retail trade), the Jews' status was very liberal; by 1657 they could describe themselves as Dutch subjects and apply for citizenship—although their citizenship was not absolutely equal, nor hereditary.

Amsterdam continued to be strongly marked by the Sephardim, whose wealth and culture eclipsed that of the Ashkenazim[1] at that time. After the Cossack massacres led by the hetman Chmielnicki in Poland (1648–1651), Ashkenazim took refuge in Amsterdam and soon outnumbered the Sephardim. The most famous of the Jews in Holland was Spinoza (1632–1677). He was excommunicated by the Amsterdam synagogue for his unorthodox views in 1656. His *Ethics*, like much of his work, was only published after his death. It was from Amsterdam that Jews reached Curaçao and Surinam and from there New Amsterdam (1654)—soon to become New York—and Newport (Rhode Island).

Marranos began settling in Antwerp, Hamburg, and Amsterdam in the sixteenth century and slightly later in London, where there were several hundred under Charles I in 1648. Others settled in Bordeaux and Bayonne.

1. Ashkenazim: literally, "Germans." Yiddish-speaking Jews (speaking Judaeo-German) with a specific rite. Following the persecutions suffered in western Europe in the Middle Ages, the Ashkenazim took refuge in central and eastern Europe (see below).

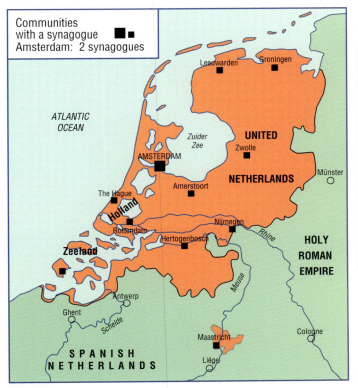

Communities
with a synagogue   ■■ ■
Amsterdam: 2 synagogues

ATLANTIC
OCEAN

Leeuwarden   Groningen

Zuider
Zee   UNITED

AMSTERDAM   Zwolle

                    NETHERLANDS   Münster

The Hague   Amerstoort
Holland
Rotterdam   Nijmegen
                                    Rhine
Hertogenbosch   HOLY
Zeeland   ROMAN
                                   EMPIRE

                    Meuse

Antwerp

Ghent
        Schelde   Maastricht   Cologne

SPANISH   Liége
NETHERLANDS

Rembrandt's engraving of a synagogue, 1648. Amsterdam, collection of the ▲
Museum Het Rembrandthius (Amsterdam, Rijksmuseum-Stitching,
Photo © the Museum).

◀ JEWISH COMMUNITIES IN THE NETHERLANDS

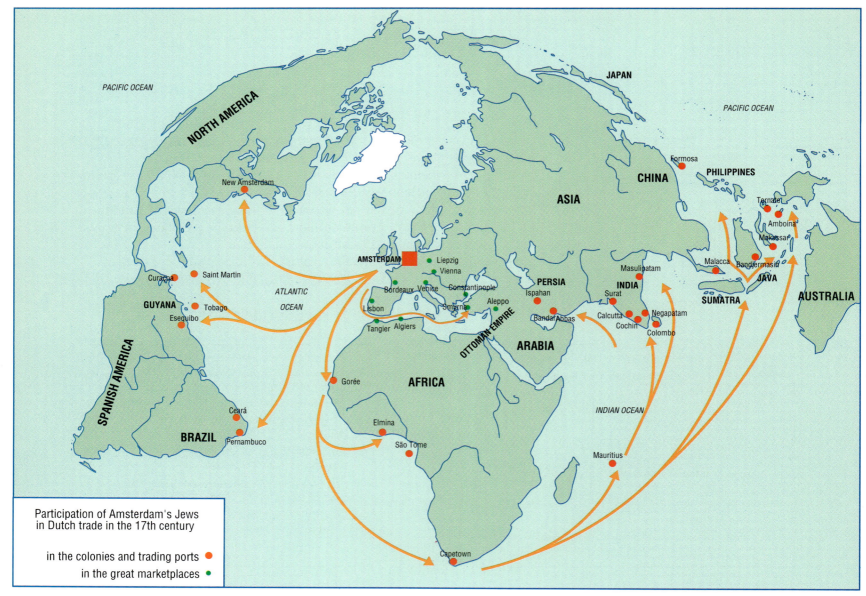

PACIFIC OCEAN

JAPAN

PACIFIC OCEAN

NORTH AMERICA

CHINA

PHILIPPINES

Formosa

ASIA

Ternate

Amboina

Makassar

AMSTERDAM ● Liepzig

● Vienna

Masulipatam

Malacca

Bandjermasin

New Amsterdam

Curaçao ● Saint Martin

Bordeaux ● Venice

● Constantinople

PERSIA

INDIA

SUMATRA

JAVA

AUSTRALIA

GUYANA

ATLANTIC

Ispahan

Surat

Tobago

OCEAN

Smyrna

● Aleppo

Lisbon

Bandar Abbas

Calcutta

Negapatam

Esequibo

SPANISH AMERICA

Tangier

Algiers

OTTOMAN EMPIRE

ARABIA

Cochin

Colombo

Ceará

Gorée

AFRICA

Pernambuco

Elmina

São Tomé

BRAZIL

INDIAN OCEAN

Mauritius

Capetown

Participation of Amsterdam's Jews
in Dutch trade in the 17th century

in the colonies and trading ports ●

in the great marketplaces ●

▲ AMSTERDAM JEWS AND INTERNATIONAL TRADE

ENGLAND After Holland, it was in Great Britain that the Marranos, and more generally the Sephardim of Portugal and Spain, played an important role.

A petition was presented to Cromwell in 1655 asking that Jews be permitted to once again settle in the country.

From the second half of the seventeenth century the Jews of England were not subject to any restrictions on their activities or particular obligations with regard to residence or clothing.

If the seventeenth century was the century of the Sephardim in Europe, the eighteenth saw the rise of the Ashkenazim, who were to dominate the following century.

The city Jews of Great Britain were organized by the two communities:

1500	Creation of a yeshiva at Cracow (Poland).
1532–1544	Luther's pamphlets first for, then against, the Jews.
1586	The Jews of Poland establish the Council of Four Lands.
1642	Six hundred Amsterdam Jews settle in Pernambuco.
1648	Intensification of massacres of Jews in Poland by the hetman Chmielnicki's Cossacks.
1655	Cromwell is asked to allow Jews to settle in England.
1677	Death of Spinoza (b. 1632), Jewish philospher born in Amsterdam to a family from Spain.

	Excommunicated by the synagogue in 1656 for his heretical views. With Philo of Alexandria and Maimonides, Spinoza is one of the very greatest figures produced by Judaism.
1750	Frederick II grants privileges to the Jews of Prussia.
1773	Gustavus III allows Jews to settle in Stockholm and Götheborg.
1782	Emperor Joseph II of Austria publishes an edict of tolerance for the Jews.
1784	Louis XVI abolishes the head tax on the Jews of Alsace.

those of Portuguese origin engaged in trade with Latin America, while the Ashkenazim specialized in trade with India.

The Jews played an important role in various German states and in the Austrian Empire. The Court Jews (*Hofjuden*) became a sort of institution, although they had no rights, since they depended on the good will of the ruler.

THE FRENCH REVOLUTION

But the great event of the eighteenth century was the French Revolution, which granted Jews political equality and full citizenship (1791).

The Batavian Republic was established in the Netherlands in 1795 and all citizens were declared equal there.

In 1796 Napoleon intervened in Italy and the gates of the ghettos were torn down. He then freed the Jews of Italy.

In 1808 the kingdom of Westphalia, under Napoleonic rule, granted citizenship to the Jews. This example was followed by Baden, then by the Confederation of the Rhine. The Free Cities of the north—Hamburg, Bremen, and Lübeck—and the states of Mecklenburg and Prussia, occupied by French forces, also granted equality in 1811 and 1812.

However, Bavaria, Saxony, and Austria rejected any change and retained their ghettos.

The revolutionary wave of 1848 led to the partial or complete emancipation of the Jews in Sweden, Denmark, Austria, and Greece.

Full equality was granted in Britain in the late nineteenth century, and in Austria in 1867. Equality was also extended in Italy in 1870. The 1871 constitution of the German Empire gave the Jews of the Reich full citizenship.

Emancipation of the Jews in Europe 1789–1914 (underlined: European states in 1878)

France (1)	1791	(1) The emancipation decree was voted by the National Assembly on 21 September 1791.
Netherlands	1797	
Venetian Republic	1797	Under pressure from Revolutionary and Imperial France (1793–1815), the Jews won equality of civil rights in Italy and the Netherlands ("sister republics") and in some states of the Empire (Westphalia, 1807; Mecklenburg, Hamburg, Bremen, Lübeck, Mainz, etc., 1808). These achievements were reversed after the fall of Napoleon.
Belgium	1830	
Hesse-Cassel	1833	
Brunswick (2)		
Kingdom of Piedmont (2)	1848	
Denmark	1848	
Kingdom of Prussia (2)	1850	(2) It was only with the rise of Liberalism after 1830 in the Empire and 1848 in Italy that emancipation was granted in various states (Hesse, Prussia, the Kingdom of Piedmont, etc.). Full emancipation of the Jews throughout the German Empire and the Kingdom of Italy was achieved in 1870–1871.
Norway (Swedish prov.)	1851	
United Kingdom (3)	1858	
Baden (2)	1862	
Sweden	1865	
Kingdom of Saxony (2)	1867	(3) In Britain progress occurred in stages: 1858, Jews allowed to sit in Parliament; 1870, right to attend university; 1890, full emancipation.
Austro-Hungarian Empire	1867	
Kingdom of Italy	1870	
German Empire	1871	(4) Emancipation imposed by Bismarck and Disraeli at the Congress of Berlin.
Switzerland	1874	
Serbia (4)		
Greece (4)	1878	
Bulgaria (4)		In 1914 Jews still had no rights in Spain, Romania, and Russia.

38

Prague's Jewish cemetery ▶
(Photo © Hulton Picture
Company).

The Ashkenazim

Faced with persecution toward the end of the Middle Ages, German-speaking Jews of German origin moved toward central Europe: Bohemia, Moravia, Poland, Lithuania. Rabbi Loeb, the "Maharil of Prague," was received at the court of Rudolf II, who welcomed the astronomer Johannes Kepler at the end of the sixteenth century. But it was Poland more than Prague that was the heart of Ashkenazi Judaism. From as early as the fourteenth century Jews there enjoyed a particularly auspicious situation and extensive prerogatives. In the seventeenth century, after Holland, it was in the area known as the "Council of Four Lands" that they enjoyed the most favorable status. This area, with such urban centers as Poznan, Cracow, and Lublin, stretched from Danzig to part of Ukraine and covered western Poland, known then in its heyday as the "Kingdom of the Two Seas" (the Baltic and the Black seas). After 1650, the massacres perpetrated by the Cossacks led to a flight back to western Europe, England, and America.

The situation was different in eastern Europe, Russia prohibited Jews from going farther east than Kiev. But with the partition and annexation of Poland in 1795,[1] Russia inherited the largest Jewish community in the world at the time. The Jews continued to be confined to a belt of territory running from the Baltic to the Black Sea. This zone comprised the Polish provinces, Lithuania, Ukraine,[2] southern Byelorussia, and Crimea.

Under the tsars and especially after 1825, under Nicholas I, the situa-

RUSSIA

1. It was in the seventeenth century that the Hassidic sect appeared in Poland.

2. Some cities, such as Kiev, were closed to them within this area.

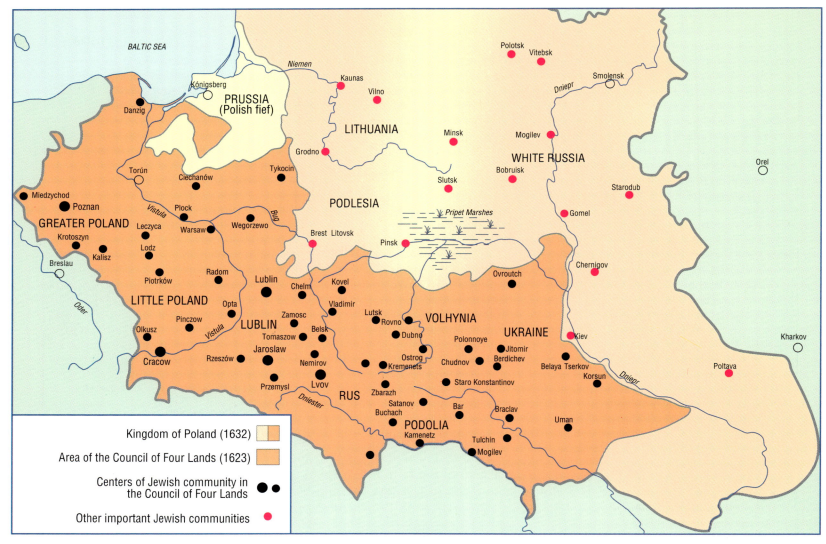

BALTIC SEA

PRUSSIA
(Polish fief)

LITHUANIA

WHITE RUSSIA

Orel

Königsberg

Danzig

Miedzychod
Poznan
GREATER POLAND
Krotoszyn
Kalisz
Breslau
Piotrków
LITTLE POLAND
Olkusz
Pinczow
Cracow
Rzeszów
Przemysl

Torún
Ciechanów
Plock
Leczyca
Warsaw
Lodz
Radom
Opta
Vistula
Jaroslaw
Lvov

Tykocin
Wegorzewo

Kaunas
Vilno

Minsk

Slutsk

PODLESIA

Grodno

Brest Litovsk

Pinsk

Pripet Marshes

Polotsk Vitebsk

Smolensk

Mogilev

Bobruisk

Starodub

Gomel

Chernigov

Kharkov

Lublin
Chelm
Zamosc
Belsk
Tomaszow
Nemirov
RUS
Zbarazh
Satanov
Buchach
Kamenetz

Kovel
Vladimir
Lutsk
Rovno
Dubno
Ostrog
Kremenets
Staro Konstantinov
Bar
Mogilev

VOLHYNIA

Ovroutch

UKRAINE

Kiev

Poltava

Polonnoye
Chudnov
Jitomir
Berdichev
Braclav
Tulchin

Belaya Tserkov
Korsun
Uman

PODOLIA

Niemen

Vistula

Bug

Oder

Dniester

Dniepr

Dniepr

LUBLIN

Kingdom of Poland (1632)	
Area of the Council of Four Lands (1623)	
Centers of Jewish community in the Council of Four Lands	● ●
Other important Jewish communities	●

▲ Jews in the Kingdom of Poland

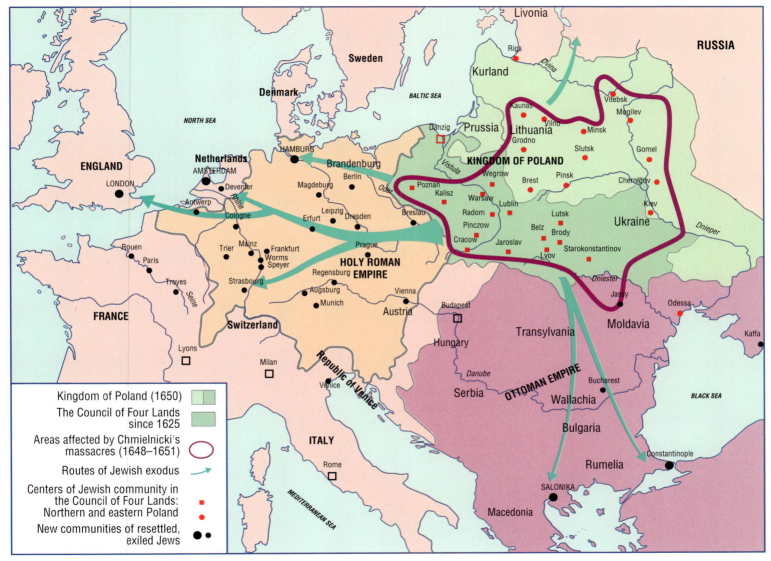

RUSSIA

Livonia

Sweden

Kurland

Riga

Denmark

BALTIC SEA

NORTH SEA

Prussia

Danzig

Vitebsk

Kaunas

Mogilev

Vilno

Minsk

Lithuania

Grodno

Slutsk

Gomel

KINGDOM OF POLAND

Netherlands

HAMBURG

Brandenburg

ENGLAND

AMSTERDAM

Berlin

Wegrow

Deventer

Magdeburg

Poznan

Brest

Pinsk

Chernigov

LONDON

Antwerp

Oder

Kalisz

Kiev

Leipzig

Cologne

Erfurt

Dresden

Breslau

Warsaw

Lublin

Ukraine

Rouen

Trier

Mainz

Frankfurt

Radom

Lutsk

Dnieper

Paris

Worms

Prague

Pinczow

Belz

Brody

Speyer

Cracow

Jaroslav

Starokonstantinov

Troyes

Strasbourg

Lvov

HOLY ROMAN

EMPIRE

Seine

Regensburg

Dniester

Augsburg

Vienna

Jassy

Munich

Switzerland

Austria

Moldavia

Odessa

FRANCE

Budapest

Kaffa

Lyons

Transylvania

Hungary

Milan

ITALY

Danube

OTTOMAN EMPIRE

Bucharest

BLACK SEA

Serbia

Wallachia

Rome

Bulgaria

Rumelia

Constantinople

MEDITERRANEAN SEA

Venice

Republic of Venice

Rhine

Vistula

Kingdom of Poland (1650)

The Council of Four Lands
since 1625

Areas affected by Chmielnicki's
massacres (1648–1651)

Routes of Jewish exodus

Centers of Jewish community in
the Council of Four Lands:
Northern and eastern Poland

New communities of resettled,
exiled Jews

SALONIKA

Macedonia

PERSECUTION OF CENTRAL EUROPEAN JEWS IN THE SEVENTEENTH CENTURY ▲

tion of the Jews of Russia was very bad. The tsar ordered that male children be taken from their families at the age of twelve, undergo a period of training up to the age of eighteen, and then be sent for military service. In Ukraine, the accusation of ritual murder was once again raised in the 1830s.

The situation improved under tsar Alexander II (1855–1881). The conscription of Jewish children at twelve was abolished, and military service reduced from twenty-five to six years for all subjects.

After the assassination of the tsar in 1881, the situation in Russia drastically worsened. There were many pogroms.

The laws of May 1882 banned Jews from any new settlement even in the traditionally authorized provinces. A *numerus clausus* was imposed on Jews in Russian schools and universities. Most of the Jews in Moscow were expelled, as were those of Saint Petersburg and Kharkov.

In 1903 there was a pogrom at Kishinev, the capital of Bessarabia.

After 1905 pogroms were part of the technique of government. Yet the economic role of Jews remained important in the nineteenth century in Russia, Romania, and, to a lesser extent, Hungary.

The massive exodus westward began in 1881, following the first pogroms, and only ended when historical circumstances no longer allowed it (closure of what had become the Soviet Union). The Jews of the Russian Empire—and those of Romania—left eastern Europe and went to the New World (Canada, Argentina, and above all the United States) or western Europe (Germany, France, and especially Britain, which played a pivotal role).

The Jews in the Russian Empire ca. 1880

5,200,000 (4.15% of the total population of the empire) distributed geographically:

A. *In the area of the Pale of Settlement* (created in western Russia after 1825)

    4,900,000 total: 1,420,000   in Ukraine
                   1,320,000   in Poland
                     730,000   in Byelorussia
                     700,000   in Lithuania
                     500,000   in New Russia
                     230,000   in Bessarabia-Moldavia

B. *In the rest of the Empire*

270,000 distributed in a number of cities in Russia, the Baltic countries (80,000), the lands of the Caucasus and central Asia (Samarkand, Bukhara).
The main urban Jewish communities:
Saint Petersburg (21,000), Kharkov (14,000), Smolensk (11,000), Moscow (10,000), Baku (12,000), Tbilisi (10,000), Irkutsk (8,500).

Pale of Settlement (1825–1917)   **Russian empire in the 19th century**

Jewish population of 40,000 and over ●

Jewish population of 20,000 and over •

Main cities forbidding Jewish residency ■

Main gateway of Jewish emigration (1800–1914) ✳

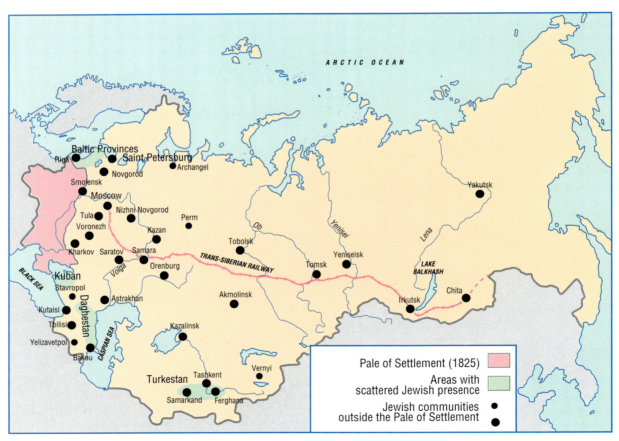

▲ Jewish Communities in Russia

The synagogue of Tbilisi in Georgia (Photo © Roch Chaliand-Minces). ▲

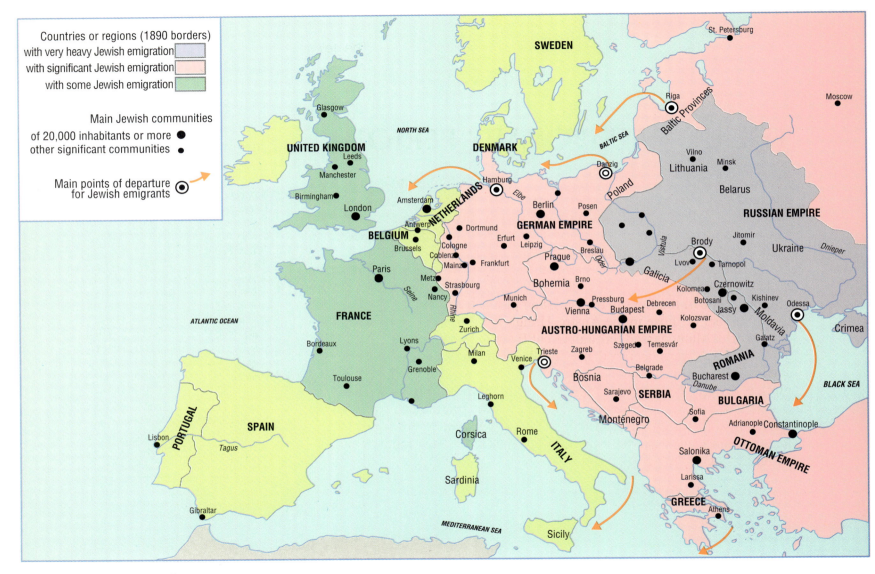

Legend:

Countries or regions (1890 borders)
- with very heavy Jewish emigration
- with significant Jewish emigration
- with some Jewish emigration

Main Jewish communities
- of 20,000 inhabitants or more ●
- other significant communities ·

⊙→ Main points of departure for Jewish emigrants

Map labels:

SWEDEN
St. Petersburg
NORTH SEA
BALTIC SEA
Baltic Provinces
Moscow
Riga
Glasgow
Leeds
Manchester
Birmingham
London
UNITED KINGDOM
DENMARK
Danzig
Vilno
Minsk
Lithuania
Belarus
RUSSIAN EMPIRE
Amsterdam
Hamburg
Elbe
Berlin
Posen
Poland
NETHERLANDS
Antwerp
BELGIUM
Brussels
Dortmund
Cologne
Coblenz
Mainz
Erfurt
Leipzig
GERMAN EMPIRE
Breslau
Vistula
Oder
Brody
Jitomir
Ukraine
Dnieper
Frankfurt
Prague
Lvov
Tarnopol
Paris
Metz
Strasbourg
Nancy
Bohemia
Brno
Galicia
Kolomea
Czernowitz
Kishinev
Seine
Rhine
Munich
Pressburg
Vienna
Budapest
Debrecen
Botosani
Jassy
Odessa
Crimea
ATLANTIC OCEAN
FRANCE
Zurich
AUSTRO-HUNGARIAN EMPIRE
Szeged
Temesvár
Kolozsvar
Moldavia
Bordeaux
Lyons
Milan
Trieste
Zagreb
Belgrade
ROMANIA
BLACK SEA
Grenoble
Venice
Bosnia
Bucharest
Danube
Leghorn
Sarajevo
SERBIA
BULGARIA
Toulouse
Montenegro
Sofia
PORTUGAL
SPAIN
Corsica
Rome
ITALY
Adrianople
Constantinople
Lisbon
Tagus
Salonika
OTTOMAN EMPIRE
Sardinia
Larissa
Gibraltar
MEDITERRANEAN SEA
Sicily
GREECE
Athens

▲ EMIGRATION OF EUROPEAN JEWRY AT THE END OF THE NINETEENTH CENTURY

THE CONTEMPORARY PERIOD

In the nineteenth century, especially in the second half, the situation of Jews changed faster: generally, in western Europe there was legal and political emancipation. Full equality was granted. But the last quarter of the century saw the appearance and development of modern anti-Semitism, peddled in France by, among others, Edouard Drumont (*La France juive*). In eastern Europe and more particularly in Russia and Romania, anti-Semitism found violent expression in pogroms after 1880–1881 and led to large-scale migration. Some of the Jews in the tsarist empire and Romania—along with a small number of those in the Austro-Hungarian Empire—emigrated to the New World. Many passed through Great Britain. Between 1880 and 1914 a great shift westward occurred, moving the center of a large segment of the Jewish diaspora to countries that had already experienced the industrial revolution. By the eve of the world war, the United States and Britain had particularly dynamic communities. However, the importance of Jews in Germany and Austria, with their impressive elites, must not be underestimated. Central and eastern Europe continued until 1939 to predominate both culturally and numerically.

The Jews in Europe (1937)
(percent of country's population in parentheses)

Poland	3,250,000	(10.50)
Romania	800,000	(4.80)
Hungary	450,000	(5.60)
Germany*	365,000	
Czechoslovakia	360,000	(2.50)
United Kingdom	340,000	(0.70)
France	270,000	(0.40)
Austria	180,000	(2.50)
Lithuania	160,000	(7.50)
Netherlands	140,000	(2.30)
Latvia	95,000	(5.40)
Yugoslavia	75,000	(0.60)
Greece	75,000	(1.20)
Italy	50,000	(0.12)
Belgium	45,000	(0.80)
Switzerland	20,000	(1.50)
Sweden	10,000	(0.16)
U.S.S.R.** about 3,000,000		

*In 1932, 525,000 Jews in Germany.
**U.S.S.R.: 2,220,000 Jews in Ukraine and Byelorussia alone.

1868	Creation in Paris of the *Alliance Israélite Universelle.*
1881–1882	Pogroms in Russia.
1882	Leo Pinsker (1821–1891) publishes *Auto Emancipation.*
1886	Edouard Dumont publishes *La France juive,* an anti-Semitic tract.
1887	Romania bars Jews from the civil service.
1894	Beginning of the Dreyfus affair.
	Zola publishes *J'accuse.*
1896	Theodor Herzl publishes *The Jewish State.*
1897	First Zionist congress in Basel. Creation of the *Bund* (Workers' League of Lithuania, Poland, and Russia).
1903	Pogrom at Kishinev (Bessarabia).
1905	Chaim Weizmann establishes the Jewish National Fund to buy land in Palestine, where small agricultural colonies had been appearing since 1883. Several hundred pogroms occur following the aborted 1905 revolution.
1906	Rehabilitation of Captain Dreyfus.
1908	Young Turk revolution, equality of rights proclaimed.
1911–1913	Mendel Beilis accused of ritual murder in Kiev. He is acquitted after a stormy trial.
1917	Emancipation of the Jews proclaimed in Russia, but persecution during the civil war.

1917	Balfour Declaration legalizing the creation of a Jewish National Home in Palestine.
1919	Emancipation of the Jews in Romania.
	Following the war, with the wave of revolutions (in which many Jews participate), the *Protocols of the Elders of Zion,* a forgery prepared under Nicholas II at the turn of the century, has a great impact in the West.
1920–1921	Anti-Zionist disturbances in Palestine.
1933	Adolf Hitler comes to power.
1935	The Nuremberg Laws deprive Jews of their citizenship.
	Marriages between Jews and Aryans banned.
1936–1939	Guerrilla war between Zionists and Arabs in Palestine. British White Book halting Jewish immigration.
1938	"Kristallnacht" (9–10 Nov.).
1939	Establishment of ghettos in Warsaw and several other cities in German-annexed Poland.
1940	Mass deportation of Jews begins.
1942	In January, at the Wannsee conference, the plan for the "Final Solution" is adopted by Nazi leaders.
1942–1945	5.2 million Jews are killed by the Nazis during World War II.
1948	Creation of the state of Israel.

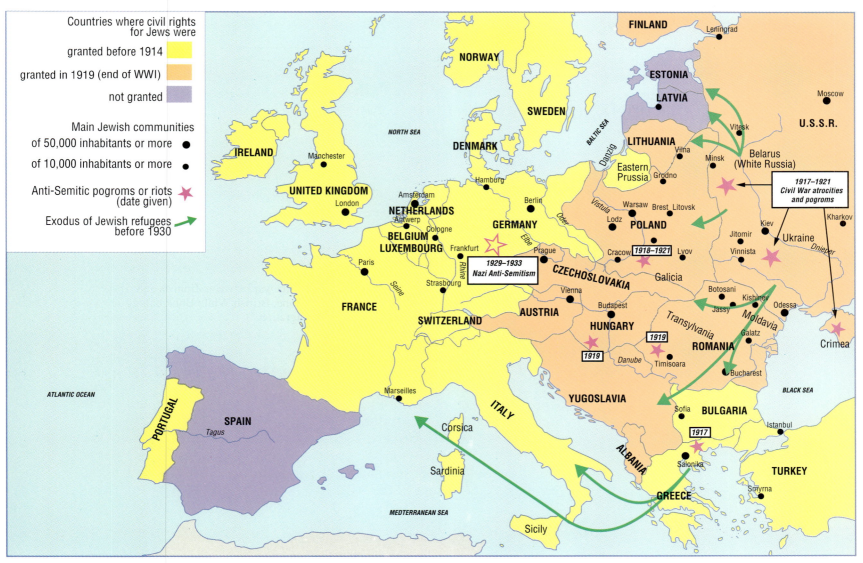

Countries where civil rights for Jews were

- granted before 1914
- granted in 1919 (end of WWI)
- not granted

Main Jewish communities
- of 50,000 inhabitants or more ●
- of 10,000 inhabitants or more •

Anti-Semitic pogroms or riots ★
(date given)

Exodus of Jewish refugees →
before 1930

NORTH SEA
BALTIC SEA
ATLANTIC OCEAN
MEDITERRANEAN SEA
BLACK SEA

FINLAND
NORWAY
SWEDEN
DENMARK
IRELAND
UNITED KINGDOM
NETHERLANDS
BELGIUM
LUXEMBOURG
GERMANY
FRANCE
SWITZERLAND
PORTUGAL
SPAIN
ITALY
AUSTRIA
HUNGARY
CZECHOSLOVAKIA
POLAND
LITHUANIA
LATVIA
ESTONIA
U.S.S.R.
Belarus (White Russia)
Ukraine
YUGOSLAVIA
ROMANIA
BULGARIA
ALBANIA
GREECE
TURKEY

Leningrad
Moscow
Manchester
London
Amsterdam
Antwerp
Cologne
Hamburg
Berlin
Frankfurt
Paris
Strasbourg
Marseilles
Vienna
Budapest
Prague
Cracow
Lodz
Warsaw
Brest Litovsk
Lyov
Danzig
Eastern Prussia
Grodno
Vilna
Minsk
Vitesk
Kiev
Kharkov
Jitomir
Vinnista
Botosani
Kishinev
Jassy
Odessa
Galatz
Bucharest
Timisoara
Sofia
Istanbul
Smyrna
Salonika
Crimea

Vistula
Oder
Elbe
Rhine
Seine
Tagus
Danube
Dnieper
Galicia
Transylvania
Moldavia
Corsica
Sardinia
Sicily

1929–1933 Nazi Anti-Semitism

1917–1921 Civil War atrocities and pogroms

1918–1921
1919
1919
1919
1917

NAZI GERMANY

From the time they came to power the German National Socialists had proclaimed their anti-Semitism, which had already been given ample expression since the creation of the party. In 1935 the Nuremberg Laws deprived Jews of their citizenship.

The rise of anti-Semitism in Germany and other countries in Europe (Romania, Hungary, and Italy, where anti-Jewish laws were issued in 1938) led tens of thousands of refugees to seek asylum in Palestine. But their coming was no more welcomed by the authorities than it was elsewhere. The British, who in 1917 had issued the Balfour Declaration, envisaging the creation of a "Jewish National Home," limited all new immigration when faced with armed resistance (1936–1939) by the Palestinian Arabs, who looked upon the Jews as foreign intruders.

During the Second World War the Jews in a Europe occupied by the troops of Germany or her allies were systematically deported—when they were not summarily liquidated, as in Russia or Ukraine in 1941–1942.

In January 1942, at the Wannsee conference, the plan for the "Final Solution" of the Jewish problem was adopted by the Nazi leaders. The death camps, where opponents of the new order were already being murdered in the 1930s, now killed 5.2 million Jews guilty simply of being Jews, as well as millions of others. Auschwitz has become the symbol of this genocide. This disaster eradicated from the map the Yiddish-speaking communities of Poland, the Baltic countries, and the whole of central Europe, as well as the Sephardic communities of the Balkans.

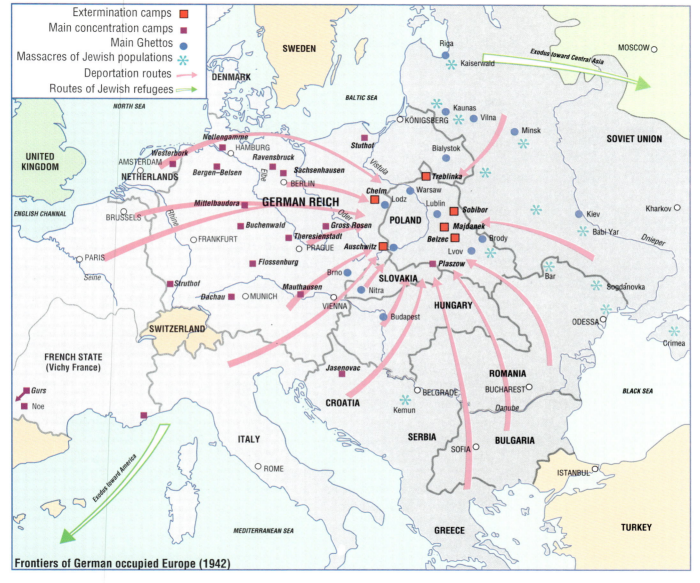

Extermination camps ■
Main concentration camps ■
Main Ghettos ●
Massacres of Jewish populations ✳
Deportation routes ➡
Routes of Jewish refugees ➡

SWEDEN

DENMARK

NORTH SEA

BALTIC SEA

Riga
✳ Kaiserwald
Exodus toward Central Asia
MOSCOW ○

Kaunas
KÖNIGSBERG ○ ✳ ● Vilna
✳ ● Minsk

SOVIET UNION

UNITED KINGDOM

AMSTERDAM ○
NETHERLANDS

Nellengamme
Westerbork
HAMBURG ○
Ravensbrück
Bergen–Belsen
Sachsenhausen
BERLIN ○

Stuthof ■

Vistula

Bialystok ●

✳ ● Treblinka
Chelm ■ ● Warsaw
● Lodz
Lublin ●
Sobibor ■
Majdanek ■
✳ Kiev ● Kharkov ○

ENGLISH CHANNAL

BRUSSELS ○

Mittelbaudora ■

GERMAN REICH

Oder

Buchenwald ■
Theresienstadt ■
Gross Rosen ■

Elbe

POLAND

Belzec ■ ● Brody

Auschwitz ■

Lvov
✳ Babi Yar
Dnieper

PARIS ○

FRANKFURT ○
PRAGUE ○
Rhine

Flossenburg ■

Seine

Brno ●

SLOVAKIA
Nitra ●

Plaszow ■

✳ Bar

Sogdánovka ✳

Struthof ■

Dachau ■ MUNICH ○
Mauthausen ■

VIENNA ○

HUNGARY

ODESSA ○

SWITZERLAND

Budapest ●

FRENCH STATE
(Vichy France)

Gurs ■
Noe ■

ROMANIA
BUCHAREST ○

BLACK SEA

Jasenovac ■

ITALY

CROATIA
✳ Kemun

BELGRADE ○

Danube

Crimea ✳

Exodus toward America

ROME ○

SERBIA

SOFIA ●

BULGARIA

MEDITERRANEAN SEA

GREECE

ISTANBUL ○

TURKEY

Frontiers of German occupied Europe (1942)

JEWS AND ARABS: FROM PALESTINE TO ISRAEL

In the aftermath of this tragedy, while the British announced their intention of leaving a Palestine where they had to face the armed violence of Zionist organizations, the United Nations adopted a plan to partition Palestine (1947). The state of Israel came into being on 14 May 1948. The next day the Arab armies entered Palestine.

Whereas in 1931 there had been 175,000 Jews out of 1,036,000 inhabitants in Palestine, on the eve of the independence of Israel they accounted for more than 40 percent of the total population.

The Sephardic diaspora—except in the Balkans and southeastern Europe—played little part in the great migrations of the years 1880 through 1914. The Jews of the Arab countries (Yemen, Iraq, Syria, Egypt, and those of North Africa) began to leave those countries in large numbers only after the creation of the state of Israel, and went mostly to North America, Israel, or France. Generally, the Jews in other Muslim countries where ancient communities remained, like Iran or Turkey, tended to emigrate.

While the diaspora of "Oriental" Jews left the Arab countries, a very ancient Jewish community continued, however, to survive in Morocco. On the other hand, large numbers of Palestinians were transformed into refugees and exiles by the creation of the state of Israel.

Jews in the Arab world

	ca. 1945	ca. 1970
Algeria	140,000	1,500
Morocco	285,000	50,000
Tunisia	110,000	12,000
Libya	36,000	a few doz.
Egypt	80,000	very few
Iraq	135,000	2,300
Syria	30,000	3,000
Yemen	55,000	500
Lebanon	10,000	9,000
Aden	7,000	0

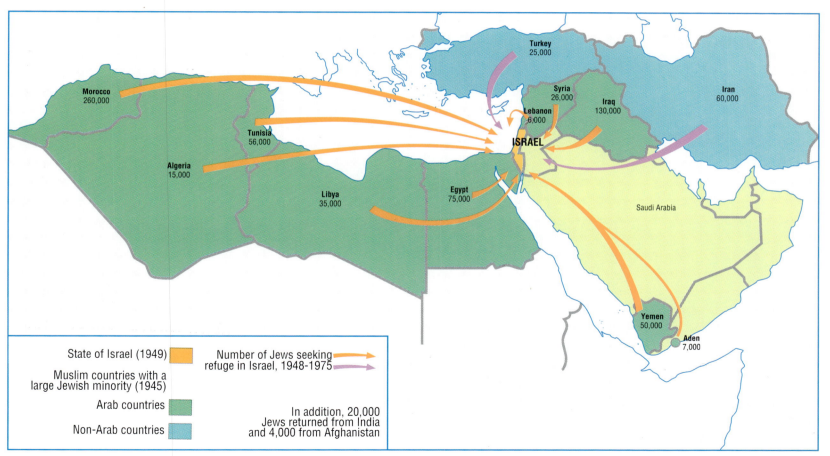

Morocco
260,000

Tunisia
56,000

Algeria
15,000

Libya
35,000

Egypt
75,000

Turkey
25,000

Syria
26,000

Lebanon
6,000

Iraq
130,000

Iran
60,000

ISRAEL

Saudi Arabia

Yemen
50,000

Aden
7,000

State of Israel (1949)

Muslim countries with a
large Jewish minority (1945)

Arab countries

Non-Arab countries

Number of Jews seeking
refuge in Israel, 1948-1975

In addition, 20,000
Jews returned from India
and 4,000 from Afghanistan

MOVEMENT OF JEWS IN ARABIC COUNTRIES TO ISRAEL ▲

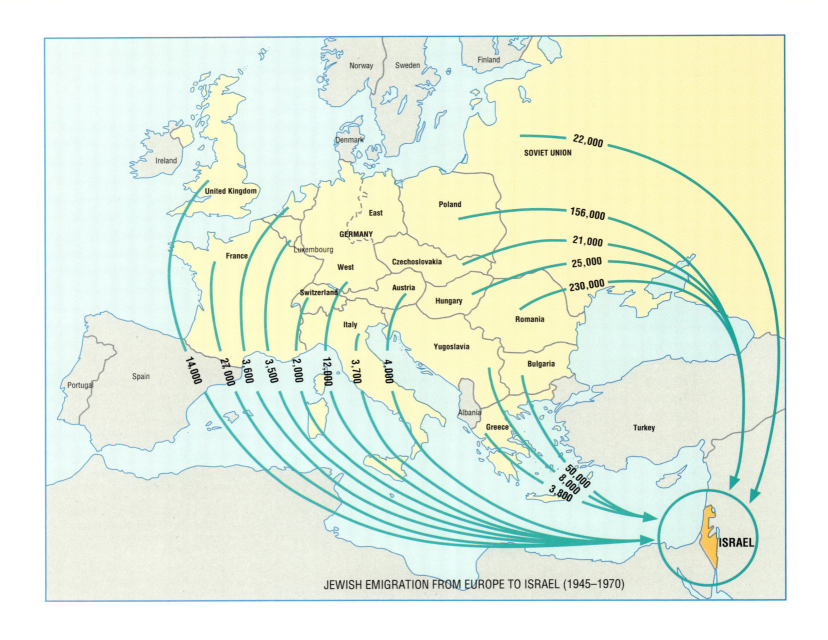

Norway
Sweden
Finland

Ireland

Denmark

United Kingdom

SOVIET UNION

Poland

East
GERMANY

Luxembourg

France

West

Czechoslovakia

Switzerland

Austria

Hungary

Italy

Romania

Yugoslavia

Bulgaria

Portugal

Spain

Albania

Greece

Turkey

22,000
156,000
21,000
25,000
230,000

14,000
27,000
3,600
3,500
2,000
12,000
3,700
4,000

50,000
8,000
3,800

ISRAEL

JEWISH EMIGRATION FROM EUROPE TO ISRAEL (1945–1970)

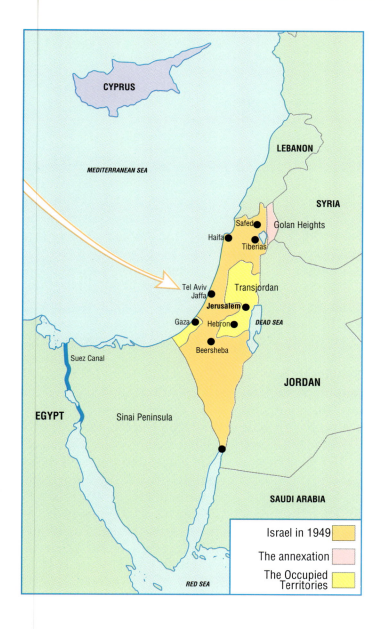

CYPRUS

LEBANON

MEDITERRANEAN SEA

SYRIA

Safed

Golan Heights

Haifa

Tiberias

Tel Aviv
Jaffa

Transjordan

Jerusalem

Gaza

Hebron

DEAD SEA

Beersheba

Suez Canal

JORDAN

EGYPT

Sinai Peninsula

SAUDI ARABIA

RED SEA

Israel in 1949	
The annexation	
The Occupied Territories	

◀ ISRAEL AND THE OCCUPIED
   TERRITORIES SINCE 1967

After the creation of the state of Israel, the movement of "return" intensified particularly from the Arab countries, where hostility toward Israel was total. This migratory movement continues today from the Soviet Union.

Meanwhile, in 1948 and 1967, large numbers of Palestinians were transformed into refugees—mostly in neighboring countries. The status of the West Bank and Gaza, where the Palestinians have been showing their hostility to the occupation for several years, had been uncertain for years, until an agreement was reached in 1993 on Gaza and Jericho between Israel and the P.L.O.

◀ Previous page: THE MOVEMENT OF
   THE JEWS OF EUROPE TO ISRAEL
   (1945–1970)

THE JEWS IN THE UNITED STATES

Today, the major receiving country of the Jewish diaspora is undoubtedly the United States (with a Jewish population almost twice that of Israel).[1] The American Jewish diaspora plays an essential role both in world Judaism and in national life. Between the late nineteenth century and the middle of the twentieth the Jewish diaspora underwent a major shift from the Slav to the Anglo-Saxon world; 5.2 million Jews, meanwhile, disappeared during the Second World War.

The Jews represent less than 3 percent of the American population, and 85 percent of the Jewish community is concentrated in the biggest cities. New York alone has over two thirds of the total Jewish population of the United States. The other important cities are Los Angeles and Chicago.

The Jews were present as colonists in New England from as early as 1654 (coming from Brazil). But it was only in 1728 that they obtained the right to build a synagogue in New York. A hundred years later, in 1825, the total Jewish population of the United States still barely exceeded five thousand. This first wave was totally Sephardic.

Brown University (Rhode Island), the University of Pennsylvania, and King's College (today Columbia University) in New York accepted Jewish students. In 1787 the Constitutional Convention declared that there should be no religious criteria for holding public office in the United States. Between 1880 and 1914, the pogroms and persecutions of all sorts as well as economic conditions in Europe led to large numbers of arrivals.

Almost two million Jews settled in the United States in those three decades. By 1917, the year the nation entered World War I, the American Jewish community numbered some 3,400,000.

1. The total world Jewish population is estimated to be 18 million. The United States has 6 million, of whom 2.2 million live in New York and 0.6 in Los Angeles.

DOMINION OF CANADA

Lake Superior

Lake Michigan

Lake Huron

Lake Erie

MONTREAL

Milwaukee
Chicago
Fort Wayne
Lafayette
Cincinnati
Saint Louis
Louisville
Denver
Coloma
San Francisco

Rochester
Syracuse
Buffalo
Cleveland
Wilkes Barre
Pittsburgh
Danville
Lancaster
Wheeling
Baltimore

Albany
New Haven
Easton
NEW YORK
Newark
PHILADELPHIA

Boston
NEWPORT (1680)

EUROPEAN JEWS

C O L O N I E S

THE THIRTEEN ORIGINAL

RICHMOND
Norfolk

ATLANTIC OCEAN

Columbia
Augusta
CHARLESTON

Vicksburg
Montgomery
Natchez
Mobile
Donaldsonville
New Orleans

SAVANNAH

GULF OF MEXICO

FLORIDA
(Spain)

United States in 1800

Sephardic communities established in the 18th century

Other Jewish communities (1800–1850)

Sephardic immigration

Other Jewish immigration (1800–1850)

Jews in the United States

1790	1,500
1800	2,000
1826	6,000
1840	15,000
1848	50,000
1860	100,000
1878	230,000
1907	1,177,000
1927	4,230,000
1955	4,975,000
1980	5,690,000
1990	6,200,000

◀ EARLY JEWISH ARRIVALS IN NORTH AMERICA

The quota policy instituted in the 1920s slowed down the numbers of such arrivals but favored immigration from western European countries, especially Germany.

In the beginning the great majority of Jewish immigrants formed a wretched industrial proletariat in New York, Boston, Philadelphia, and Chicago. After 1900, there were more craftsmen, especially in textiles. In the 1920s the cinema became an industry to which American Jews made a significant contribution. In the 1930s the proportion of proletarianized Jews was falling sharply. Schooling, highly encouraged, was one means of moving up into the professions. After the Second World War Jews were one of the most prosperous groups in the country.

Over the period 1880–1945 anti-Semitism in the United States was less strong than in the countries of democratic western Europe, yet there were anti-Semitic campaigns at the end of the nineteenth century and in the 1920s and '30s. It must not be forgotten that in the 1930s, Jews driven out by the Nazis were seeking a haven but were refused in most countries, including the United States. Some clubs practiced discrimination until the end of the 1950s; some residential areas remained closed to Jews until after the Second World War. Today, the Jewish community in the United States is both remarkably integrated and politically powerful.

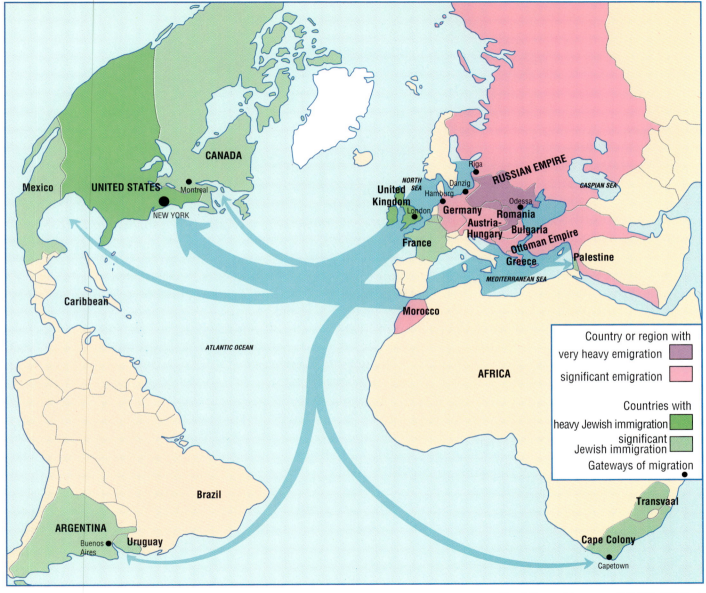

CANADA

Montreal

UNITED STATES

NEW YORK

Mexico

Caribbean

ATLANTIC OCEAN

Brazil

ARGENTINA

Buenos
Aires

Uruguay

RUSSIAN EMPIRE

Riga

Danzig

Hamburg

NORTH
SEA

United
Kingdom

London

Germany

France

Austria-
Hungary

Romania

Odessa

Bulgaria

Ottoman Empire

Greece

Palestine

CASPIAN SEA

MEDITERRANEAN SEA

Morocco

AFRICA

Transvaal

Cape Colony

Capetown

Country or region with

very heavy emigration

significant emigration

Countries with

heavy Jewish immigration

significant
Jewish immigration

Gateways of migration

THE "GRAND MIGRATION" (1880–1914) ▲

Emigration of Jews outside Europe (1880–1939)
(in thousands)

	1881–1900	1901–1914	1915–1930	1931–1939
United States	675	1,375	415	110
Canada	10	95	50	15
South Africa	23	20	15	10
Palestine	30	40	115	250
Latin America	27	100	145	85

or 73% to North America, 12% to Palestine, 10% to Latin America, 5% to the rest of the world.

Hester Street on New York's Lower East Side, ▶
circa 1900 (Museum of the City of New York.
Photo © the Museum).

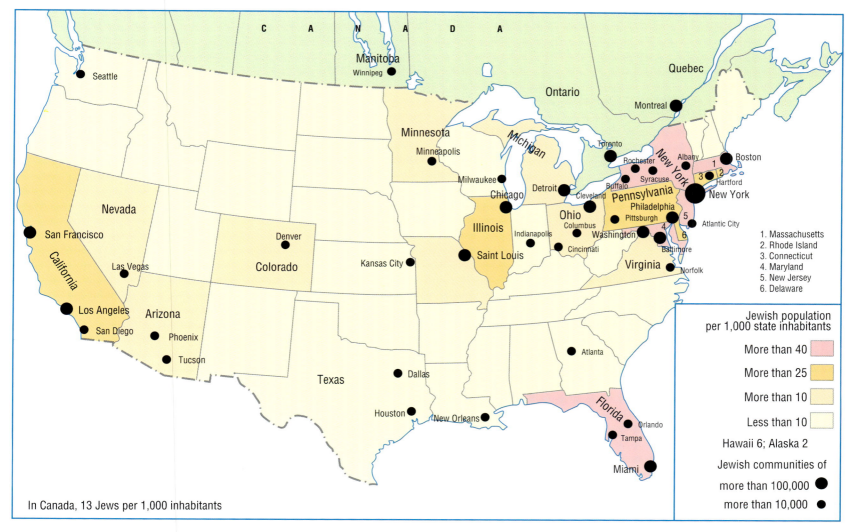

Jewish population per 1,000 state inhabitants

- More than 40
- More than 25
- More than 10
- Less than 10

Hawaii 6; Alaska 2

Jewish communities of

more than 100,000 ●

more than 10,000 •

1. Massachusetts
2. Rhode Island
3. Connecticut
4. Maryland
5. New Jersey
6. Delaware

In Canada, 13 Jews per 1,000 inhabitants

JEWS IN THE MODERN UNITED STATES AND CANADA ▲

Canada

Seattle · Winnipeg · Manitoba · Ontario · Quebec · Montreal

United States

Minnesota · Minneapolis · Michigan · Toronto · New York · Albany · Boston · Rochester · Hartford · Nevada · Milwaukee · Chicago · Detroit · Buffalo · Syracuse · Cleveland · Pennsylvania · New York · San Francisco · California · Illinois · Denver · Ohio · Columbus · Philadelphia · Pittsburgh · Atlantic City · Las Vegas · Colorado · Indianapolis · Washington · Kansas City · Saint Louis · Cincinnati · Baltimore · Virginia · Los Angeles · Arizona · Norfolk · San Diego · Phoenix · Tucson · Texas · Dallas · Atlanta · Houston · New Orleans · Florida · Orlando · Tampa · Miami

THE JEWS IN THE U.S.S.R.

After the United States and Israel, the former Soviet Union is the country with the largest number of Jews: some 2.5 million in 1988, mainly in Russia, Ukraine, and Belarus. There were significant minorities in Uzbekistan, Moldavia, the Baltic republics, and Georgia.

Until recently, there was significant discrimination against Jews: there were no community institutions and no cultural rights although Jews were recognized as one of the country's national groups. These conditions contrasted with those introduced in the immediate aftermath of the revolution, which were very good compared to the tsarist period: both Yiddish-speaking Jewish culture and Jewish artists integrated into Russian cultural life could express themselves freely.

Stalinism struck the Jews as it did the rest of Soviet society in the 1930s, but after the war this repression took on a much more overtly anti-Semitic slant.

Though improving somewhat under Krushchev, the situation worsened again after 1970. The number of departures (difficult to ascertain) rose. Officially there were 1,810,000 Jews in the 1979 census.[1]

Most of the Jews in the Soviet Union are Ashkenazim, but the Jewish community in Georgia has been settled in the region since antiquity. In the Caucasus (Azerbaijan) there were "mountain Jews." In central Asia, Jews whose language is Tadzhik (related to Persian) were established in Samarkand, Bukhara, Dyuchambe, and Tashkent. A very large proportion of Jews have left the former Soviet Union since the mid-1980s, many of them for Israel.

1. Estimates often put their number at that date at 2.5 to 3 million. Jewish emigration from the U.S.S.R.: 24,000 between 1948 and 1970, 242,000 between 1970 and 1980, 600,000(?) between 1980 and 1992.

FINLAND

BALTIC SEA

Lake Ladoga

Tallin

LENINGRAD

ESTONIA

Perm

Riga

LATVIA

LITHUANIA

Kaunas

Kaliningrad

Vilna

Grodno

Dvina

Vitebsk

Smolensk

Gorki

Kazan

Ufa

URALS

MOSCOW

Minsk

Mogilev

RUSSIAN SOVIET FEDERATED SOCIALIST REPUBLIC

Kuibyshev

BYELORUSSIA

Gomel

Bryansk

POLAND

Chernigov

Kursk

Orenburg

Saratov

Jitomir

KIEV

Voronezh

Lvov

Berdichev

Vinnista

UKRAINE

Kharkov

KAZAKHSTAN

Chernovsky

Dniester

Dniepropetrovsk

Donets

Volga

MOLDOVA

Kishinev

ODESSA

Kherson

Rostov

Don

Ural

ROMANIA

Simferopol

Krasnodar

Sebastopol

CRIMEA

BLACK SEA

CAUCASUS

Grozny

CASPIAN SEA

Sukhumi

Kutaisi

Derbent

Batumi

Tbilsi

GEORGIA

ARMENIA

Kirovabad

Baku

TURKEY

Yerevan

AZERBAIJAN

Jewish urban centers

over 100,000 inhabitants

over 10,000 inhabitants

significant numbers
(several thousand)

Regions with significant,
scattered Jewish communities

MODERN JEWS IN THE FORMER SOVIET UNION ▲

THE AUTONOMOUS REGION OF ▶
BIROBIDJAN

In the late 1920s Birobidjan was created to become a national home. In 1934, it was declared a Jewish oblast (autonomous region) although only 14,000 Jews lived there. In 1948 the Jewish institutions which had been created there were dissolved. At the 1970 census Birobidjan had 11,452 Jews out of a total population of some 172,000.

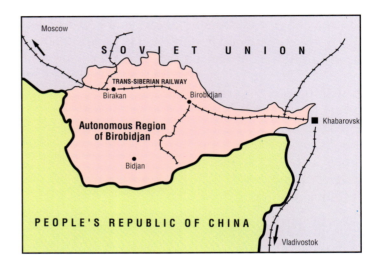

THE JEWS IN GREAT BRITAIN

There are some 450,000 Jews in Britain, and their situation has been stable since the seventeenth century. The influence of British Judaism was great in the nineteenth and early twentieth century. The Jewish community, which originally came from Holland and Germany (during the seventeenth century), was enriched by the influx of Jews from Russia between 1880 and 1920. Britain at that time was the major receiving country for Jews in Europe. The number of Jews rose from 50,000 in 1875 to about 300,000 by the time of the First World War. A new influx of immigration caused by the rise of Nazism in Germany brought the total Jewish population to almost 350,000 on the eve of the Second World War.

The integration of Jews into national life, at all levels, came gradually, pragmatically, during the second half of the nineteenth century. Since 1836 British Judaism has been represented by a Board of Deputies of British Jews.

As in the rest of Europe, Britain experienced a flare-up of anti-Semitism in the 1930s with the rise of Nazism and fascism.

The right of residence was granted to Jews by the British in 1759. The first synagogue, in Montreal, dates from 1768. In 1867 the Jewish population numbered barely a thousand. Civil equality was won in 1862. By 1920, after the great wave of immigration of 1880–1920, Canada had some 125,000 Jews (out of nine million inhabitants), mostly settled in Toronto and Montreal. Today Quebec and Ontario are home to over 80 percent of Canadian Jews. In 1919 the Canadian Jewish Congress was founded to represent the community officially. As elsewhere, the prewar period was one of immigration restrictions and manifest anti-Semitism. The restrictions remained in force until 1947. At present, the Jewish community in Canada is one of the most integrated and prosperous in the world. It has recently been strengthened with the arrival, following decolonization, of Jews from the Maghreb.

THE JEWS IN CANADA

THE JEWS IN FRANCE

Today France is home to the third largest Jewish community in the diaspora after the United States and the former Soviet Union. This community is estimated to number 600,000, half of whom live in the Paris region.

At the time of the Revolution, which emancipated the Jews (decree of 21 September 1791) by granting them full rights of citizenship, France had three groups of Jews: the first was large and Yiddish-speaking, in Alsace-Lorraine; the second, in the former region of Comtat Venaissain, the "Pope's Jews," who had long lived in ghettos; finally one in the southwest, mainly at Bordeaux, that was Sephardic, Portuguese by origin (often Marranos) and French by culture. Modern anti-Semitism manifested itself in France in the late nineteenth century and reached its peak with the Dreyfus Affair, which sharply divided the country.

The Jewish population rose significantly between the wars. Of 350,000 Jews, 200,000 were recent migrants who did not have French nationality.

In the 1930s France took in more refugees from Nazism than any other country in the world. But under the Vichy regime, the country implemented anti-Semitic measures with a zeal that sometimes outstripped that of the Nazi occupying power.

Between 1942 and 1944 almost eighty thousand Jews from France were sent to concentration camps in central Europe. Internment camps, such as the one at Gurs, were opened in France itself.

Following the Algerian war, the arrival of large numbers of Jews from North Africa and especially Algeria invigorated Jewish life in France.

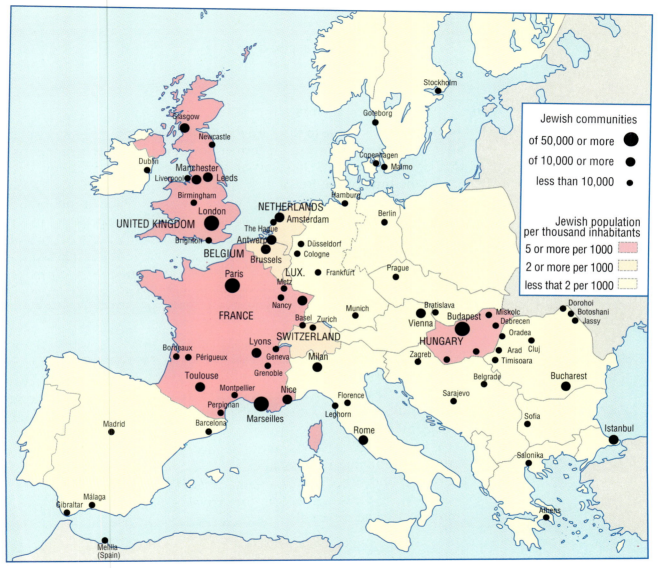

Jewish communities

- of 50,000 or more ●
- of 10,000 or more ●
- less than 10,000 ·

Jewish population per thousand inhabitants

- 5 or more per 1000
- 2 or more per 1000
- less that 2 per 1000

Stockholm

Goteborg

Copenhagen
Malmo

Glasgow

Newcastle

Dublin
Manchester
Liverpool
Leeds
Birmingham
London
Brighton

UNITED KINGDOM

Hamburg

Berlin

NETHERLANDS
Amsterdam
The Hague
Antwerp
Düsseldorf
Cologne
BELGIUM
Brussels
LUX.
Frankfurt
Prague

Paris

Metz
Nancy

FRANCE

Munich

Bratislava
Vienna
Budapest
Miskolc
Debrecen
Oradea
HUNGARY
Arad Cluj
Zagreb
Timisoara

Dorohoi
Botoshani
Jassy

Basel Zurich
SWITZERLAND
Lyons
Geneva
Milan
Grenoble
Montpellier
Nice
Bordeaux
Périgueux
Toulouse
Perpignan
Barcelona
Marseilles

Belgrade

Sarajevo

Bucharest

Florence
Leghorn
Rome

Sofia

Istanbul

Madrid

Málaga
Gibraltar

Salonika

Athens

Melilla
(Spain)

JEWS IN MODERN EUROPE ▲

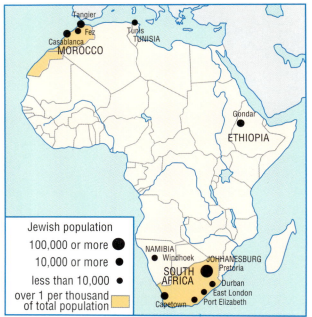

▲ JEWS IN AFRICA

◀ Ethiopian Jews in an Israeli transit center. In addition to the
Moroccan community and settlements that are a result of
modern forced dispersions, a very ancient community, that
of the Falashas, existed in Ethiopia. They have undertaken
the "return" to Israel, often under difficult conditions. (Photo
© M. Bar'am/Magnum.)

After the United States, Argentina is, with Canada, the country with the largest Jewish community in the Americas.

In the sixteenth and seventeenth centuries, Sephardim settled in Tucuman, in the far north of the country not far from the Bolivian frontier. But that community seems to have dwindled away. Here too, the great wave of immigration dates from the period 1800–1914. Some 115,000 Jews migrated to Argentina; the 1947 census counted 250,000 Jews out of a total population of 16 million, and the 1960 census gave 276,000 out of 20 million. The figures do not appear to have altered very much since then.

At the beginning of immigration, Jews from Russia tried to set up agricultural settlements. Thirty thousand of them lived the life of gauchos. But, as elsewhere, the diaspora is fundamentally an urban one.

There was strong anti-Semitic agitation in the 1930s and '40s. A new wave of anti-Semitism was detectable during the military dictatorship of 1976–1982. Three-quarters of the Jewish community live in Buenos Aires.

JEWS IN LATIN AMERICA ▶

THE JEWS IN ARGENTINA

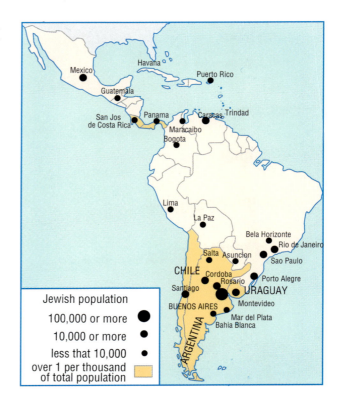

Jewish population

● 100,000 or more
• 10,000 or more
· less that 10,000
▨ over 1 per thousand of total population

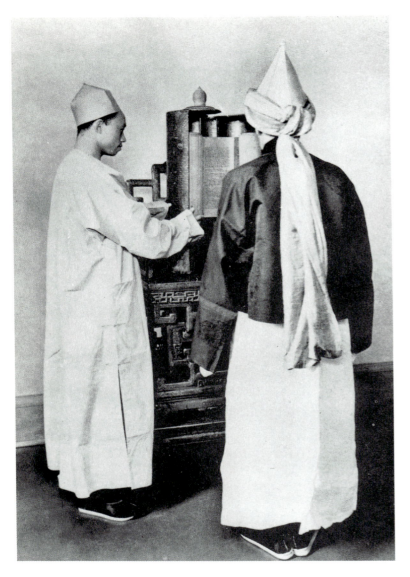

THE JEWS IN CHINA

A Jewish community long survived in Kaifeng, founded in the eleventh century by seventy families arriving from Persia. They followed the Sephardic rites. However, the presence of Jews in China goes back further. There is evidence that they were present in Canton in the eighth century. The Jews of Kaifeng built their synagogue in 1163.

Under the Mongol dynasty of Yüan (thirteenth to fourteenth centuries) there is evidence of Jewish communities in Beijing, Hangchow, Ninghsien, Nanking, and Canton. Under the Ming (fourteenth to seventeenth centuries) the situation of the small Jewish colonies was prosperous and the Chinese state was benevolent. But the community, increasingly cut off from outside Judaism, tended to lose its specific features and become more and more Sinicized. The Jesuit Matteo Ricci mentions its existence in the late sixteenth century. Under the Manchus, the attitude of the authorities ceased to be benevolent and the Jewish community's isolation and integration through loss of memory grew. By the mid-nineteenth century, when the British penetrated into China, Kaifeng had neither a rabbi nor a synagogue; but a much reduced little community still appears to survive there.

◀ Chinese Jews at the turn of the century (Photo © J.-L. Charmet).

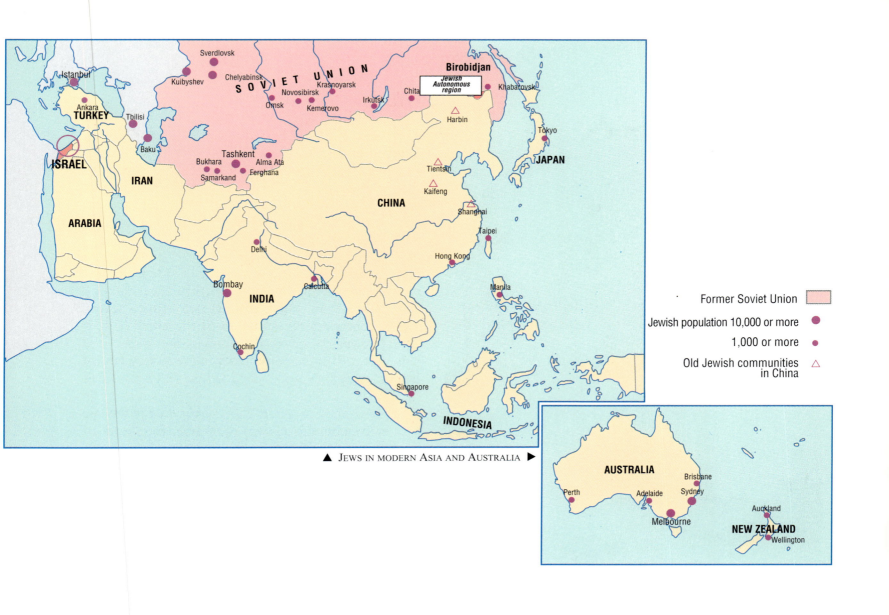

Sverdlovsk

Istanbul

Ankara
TURKEY
Tbilisi

Kuibyshev Chelyabinsk

SOVIET UNION

Birobidjan
Jewish
Autonomous
region

Krasnoyarsk

Novosibirsk

Omsk Kemerovo

Irkutsk Chita Khabarovsk

Baku

ISRAEL

IRAN

Bukhara

Samarkand

Tashkent
Alma Ata

Ferghana

ARABIA

Delhi

Bombay

INDIA

Calcutta

Cochin

Harbin

Tientsin

Kaifeng

CHINA

Shanghai

Hong Kong

Taipei

Tokyo

JAPAN

Manila

Singapore

INDONESIA

▲ JEWS IN MODERN ASIA AND AUSTRALIA ▶

Former Soviet Union

Jewish population 10,000 or more ●

1,000 or more •

Old Jewish communities △
in China

AUSTRALIA

Brisbane

Perth

Adelaide

Sydney

Melbourne

Auckland

NEW ZEALAND

Wellington

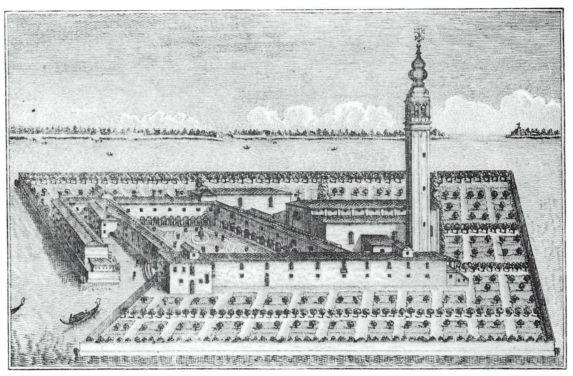

▲ The monastery of San Lazarro in Venice, a reminder of the Armenian diaspora. Engraving 1820 (Venice, Archives, Congregazione Mehitarista di San Lazarro degli Armeni).

THE ARMENIAN DIASPORA

1

Actual Communities ○
Commercial Routes —

Sinope
Pontus
BLACK SEA
Colchis
Tiflis
Sarmatia
CASPIAN SEA
Batumi
Trebizond
Kura
Baku
Cappadocia
Erzeroum
Yerevan
Artaxata
ARMENIA
Araxes
Galatia
Van
Tabriz
Tigranocerta
Lake Urmia
Tarus
Cilicia
Antioch
Edessa
Aleppo
Mosul
Parthian Kingdom
Cyprus
MEDITERRANEAN SEA
Syria
Euphrates
Tigris
Mesopotamia
Ecbatana

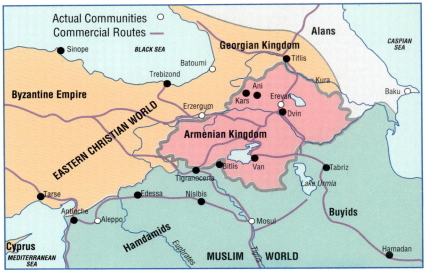

2

Actual Communities ○
Commercial Routes —

Sinope
BLACK SEA
Georgian Kingdom
Alans
CASPIAN SEA
Batoumi
Tiflis
Byzantine Empire
Trebizond
Ani
Kura
Kars
Erevan
Baku
Erzergum
Dvin
EASTERN CHRISTIAN WORLD
Armenian Kingdom
Bitlis
Van
Tabriz
Tigranocerta
Lake Urmia
Tarse
Edessa
Nisibis
Antioche
Aleppo
Mosul
Buyids
Hamdamids
Cyprus
MEDITERRANEAN SEA
Euphrates
Tigris
MUSLIM WORLD
Hamadan

3

Sinope
BLACK SEA
GEORGIAN EMPIRE
CASPIAN SEA
Tbilisi
KINGDOM OF
Trebizond
TREBIZOND
Ani
Kura
Kars
Dvin
BYZANTINE WORLD
Armenia
Araxes
Iconium
Van
Tabriz
Lake Urmia
Sis
ARMENIAN KINGDOM OF CILICIA
Tarsus
Edessa
Antioch
SELJUK EMPIRE
EASTERN LATIN STATES
Euphrates
Mosul
Cyprus
Nicosia
MEDITERRANEAN SEA

The Amenian State of Cilicia (12th–14th centuries) ▮
Amenian migrations (11th century) ⟶

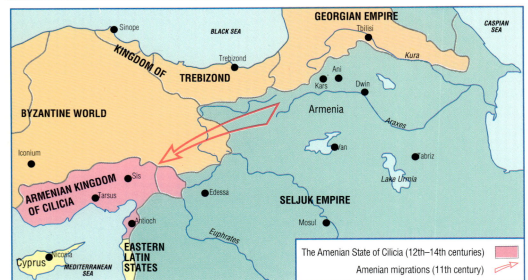

1. HISTORICAL ARMENIA
2. ARMENIA OF THE BAGRATIDS
3. THE KINGDOM OF CILICIA

A stele, or carved inscription, at Behistun, in Persia, provides historic evidence for the existence of Armenia since the fifth century B.C.

Geographically situated at one of the world's great crossroads, the Armenian people, with their Indo-European language, have experienced varying fortunes. First dominated by Persia at the time of Cyrus (Xenophon's Ten Thousand in the *Anabasis* passed through Armenia), then by Alexander the Great, the kingdom of Armenia reached its greatest territorial extent in the reign of Tigranes II (first century B.C.), extending its authority by conquest to a large part of the Middle East. Defeated by Pompey, Armenia was fought over by Rome, as well as Arsacid and Sassanid Persia. In 312 Armenia was the first state to adopt Christianity as its official religion (Saint Gregory the Illuminator), even before the conversion of the emperor Constantine. The creation of an alphabet (ca. 405) and the growth of a literature, which experienced straightaway its golden age in the fifth century, put the finishing touches to the specific features of Armenian identity.

From the seventh to the ninth centuries, Armenia was the object of a tug-of-war between Byzantium and the Arabs.

The Bagratid dynasty (885), with its capital at Ani, assured Armenia over a century and a half of exceptional prosperity until it was defeated first by Byzantium in 1045 and then by the Seljuk Turks in 1064.

HISTORIC ARMENIA

BYZANTIUM

Thousands of Armenians were deported by the Byzantine emperor Maurice (582–602) to Bulgaria, at Philippopolis (Plovdiv).[1] Subsequently, they established the Paulician heresy in Thrace which in turn inspired the Bogomil movement (eleventh to twelfth centuries), whose influence was felt as far away as the West (Cathars, Waldensians). In Plovdiv and the surrounding region these Armenians found an older Armenian community which had been living there since the fifth century.

During the eleventh and twelfth centuries Armenian churches and monasteries were very active. A large colony survived at Tirnovo (Bulgaria).

A new influx of Armenians arrived in Bulgaria after the conquest of the town of Kamenets Podolski in Ukraine by the Ottomans in 1672. Significant Armenian communities in Bulgaria survived until the twentieth century in Plovdiv, Ruse (on the Danube), Sofia, and the ports of Varna and Bourgas (on the Black Sea). The oldest Armenian diaspora is probably the one in Bulgaria.

The endless conflict between Byzantium and Armenia did not prevent the exodus to Byzantium of numerous Armenians who gave it a series of illustrious generals and emperors: Narses, the general who conquered Italy under Justinian; John Curcuas, who defeated the Arabs in the seventh century. In the eighth and ninth centuries Byzantium had four emperors of Armenian origin, including the founder of the so-called Macedonian dynasty.

1. Cf. D. M. Lang, *The Armenians: A People in Exile* (London, 1972).

The first large-scale migration of the Armenian people since the creation of the kingdom of Armenia occurred following the collapse of the Bagratid dynasty. At the end of the eleventh century (1080), a Bagratid prince established a colony in Cilicia, which in the twelfth century became a new Armenian state and retained its independence until 1375.

Part of the Armenian population—the people from Vaspouragan (an Armenian province in the area of Lake Van)—migrated in the eleventh century to Cilicia (a coastal area of southeastern Anatolia), while some of the people of Ani migrated to Crimea. Some colonies went off to settle in Hungary and Poland as well as Moldavia, and some in western Anatolia.

In Ruthenia and Galicia their settlement was favored by Prince Lev of Galicia, who founded Lvov (Lemberg) in 1270; for centuries the town became the great Armenian mecca of Ukraine and Poland.

The kingdom of Cilicia played an important role during the Crusades and in the history of the Frankish states of the East. Its last king, Leo V de Lusignan, died in Paris in 1393 and lies with the kings of France in the basilica of Saint-Denis. While a first wave of Armenian migration had dispersed to Crimea, Ukraine, and Poland following the fall of the kingdom of Armenia in the eleventh century, a second wave joined them after the fall of the kingdom of Cilicia in the fourteenth century. The church of St. Nicholas of Kamenets Podolsk dates from 1318. From Ukraine Armenians went off to settle in Romania, Poland, and Lithuania.

In Romania the Armenian church of Botoshani dates from 1350, that of Bucharest from 1581. The Armenian colonies retained their individuality there until the twentieth century. There is evidence of their presence in

THE EARLY MIGRATIONS

Moldavia, at both Suleava and Jassy, from the fourteenth to the nineteenth century and beyond.

At the beginning of the fifteenth century Armenians fought alongside Witold, Grand Duke of Lithuania, against the Teutonic Knights and took part in the battle of Tannenberg.

From Casimir the Great (1333–1370) to John III Sobieski (1674–1696), the kings of Poland regularly renewed the commercial and other privileges granted to the Armenian community.

Lvov remained the great Armenian center of central Europe. It was only in the eighteenth century that the role of the city's Armenians began to decline. But the colony survived until the beginning of the twentieth century.

In the Middle Ages, from the tenth to the beginning of the fifteenth century, there is evidence of a continuous presence of Armenian communities of traders and craftsmen (especially masons and architects) in western Europe: Venice, Marseilles, Paris, Bruges—from the thirteenth to fifteenth centuries—and London. The word *spurk*[1] in Armenian means "dispersion."

1. Of Greek origin. The Armenians also use the word *gaghut*, from the Hebrew *galut*.

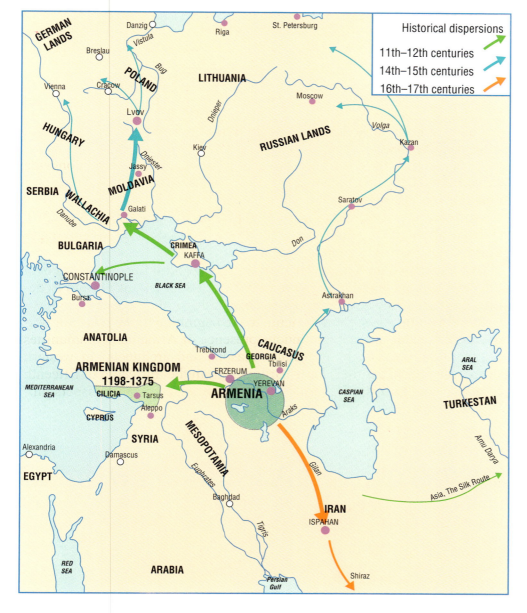

THE GREAT WAVES OF DISPERSION

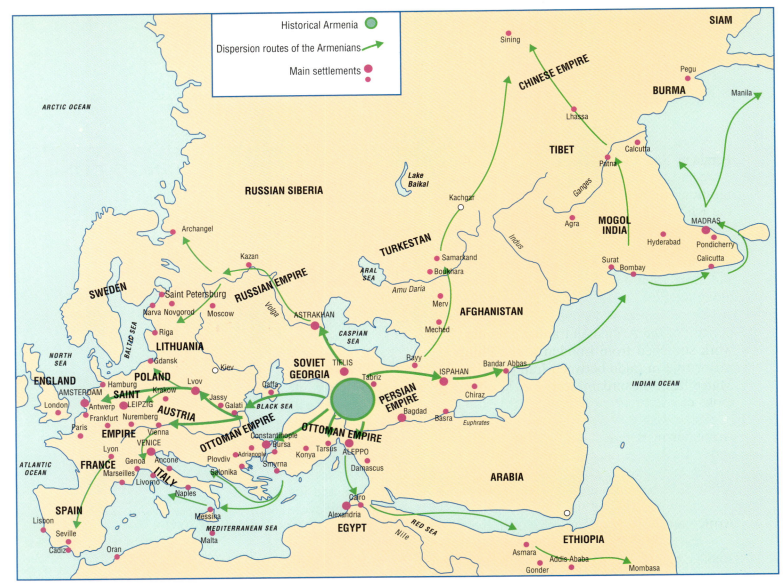

Historical Armenia

Dispersion routes of the Armenians

Main settlements

ARCTIC OCEAN

SIAM

CHINESE EMPIRE

Sining

BURMA

Pegu

Manila

Lhassa

TIBET

Calcutta

Patna

MOGOL INDIA

RUSSIAN SIBERIA

Lake Baikal

Kachgar

Ganges

Indus

MADRAS

Archangel

TURKESTAN

Samarkand

Boukhara

Agra

Hyderabad

Pondicherry

Kazan

ARAL SEA

Amu Daria

Surat

Bombay

Calicutta

SWEDEN

Saint Petersburg

Narva Novgorod

Moscow

Merv

AFGHANISTAN

Riga

Volga

ASTRAKHAN

CASPIAN SEA

Meched

INDIAN OCEAN

RUSSIAN EMPIRE

NORTH SEA

LITHUANIA

Gdansk

Kiev

Rayy

SOVIET GEORGIA

TIFLIS

Tabriz

ISPAHAN

Bandar Abbas

ENGLAND

Hamburg

POLAND

Lvov

Qaffa

PERSIAN EMPIRE

Chiraz

AMSTERDAM

SAINT

Krakow

Jassy

BLACK SEA

Bagdad

London

Antwerp

LEIPZIG

Nuremberg

Galati

AUSTRIA

Basra

Euphrates

Frankfurt

EMPIRE

Vienna

Paris

VENICE

Constantinople

Bursa

OTTOMAN EMPIRE

Konya

Tarsus

ALEPPO

Lyon

FRANCE

Genoa

Ancone

Plovdiv

Adrianople

Smyrna

Damascus

Marseilles

ITALY

Livorno

Salonika

Cairo

ARABIA

ATLANTIC OCEAN

Naples

Alexandria

SPAIN

Lisbon

Messina

EGYPT

Nile

RED SEA

Seville

MEDITERRANEAN SEA

Malta

Cadiz

Oran

ETHIOPIA

Asmara

Addis Ababa

Gonder

Mombasa

▲ THE GREAT ARMENIAN TRADING NETWORK (17TH–18TH CENT.)

In the seventeenth century several thousand Armenians were deported to Persia by Shah Abbas I. Settled near Isaphan, at New Djulfa, they prospered there and are still living there today, although a movement of Armenian emigration has been underway for several decades and has accelerated since the Khomeini revolution. In the seventeenth and eighteenth centuries this colony played a major role in trade relations between the Far East, the East, and the West. From New Djulfa, through the port of Bandar Abbas at the entry to the Persian Gulf, long-distance trade was organized by sea to India, Indonesia, and the Philippines, and by land to Tibet and China northward along the Silk Route.

The seventeenth and eighteenth centuries were the golden age of the dispersion of the Armenian trading colonies. At that time, the Armenian network stretched from London to the Philippines. The Armenians played a major role in trade between Iran (silk in particular) and Venice, Leghorn, Marseilles, Amsterdam, Antwerp, London, and Manchester. The routes they took crossed either Syria and Anatolia to the Mediterranean ports (Constantinople, etc.) or Russia to Archangel and the White Sea. In Asia, Armenian merchants found Armenian communities settled in Iraq, at Basra, and in India at Surat, Calcutta, and Madras. "What would Madras be without the Armenians?" wrote Fernand Braudel.[1] The archives of a seventeenth-century Armenian merchant,[2] which record both his travels and his dealings, show clearly that from Iran to China, by way of India and even Tibet, Armenian communities served as staging posts.

This network, which covered the Eurasian landmass, attained a considerable degree of financial power. It was dismantled by the English, and with

DEPORTATION AND TRADING COLONIES

1. F. Braudel, *Civilization and Capitalism, 15th–18th Centuries*, vol. 2, tr. Sian Reynolds (London, 1982).

2. Published by the Matenadaran Library in Yerevan; the document itself is in the Gulbenkian Foundation in Lisbon.

it the diasporas of Asia on which it was built gradually declined as well; especially from the eighteenth century the British no longer wished to deal with middlemen and took world trade directly in hand, through their colonial presence. The Indian empire installed Europe in Asia for some two centuries.

THE ARMENIANS IN ASIA

The Armenians were particularly active in Burma from the seventeenth century. They had a monopoly on rubies there, and by the end of the seventeenth century they had their own small fleet. Until the mid-eighteenth century the Armenians traded actively between Syiram (near Rangoon) and Madras. They played an important role at the court of King Alangpaya (Alompra), who unified the country between 1752 and 1760; their influence remained important there until the mid-nineteenth century. Most of them were then living at Anapura, on the river Irrawaddy between Mandalay and Ava. Their trading relations took them as far as the Moluccas and the China Sea. The advent of British control eliminated them commercially in the nineteenth century.

Although no longer occupying a dominant position in the nineteenth century, the Armenian trading diaspora in southeast Asia continued to be very active from Madras to Jakarta.

The Armenian community of Alexandria, dating from the thirteenth to fourteenth centuries, almost completely disappeared after the advent of Nasser. In Egypt under Mohammad Ali, just before the British takeover in 1882, the Armenians played a notable role in the form of two statesmen: Boghos Bey, who, as adviser to and collaborator with the Khedive (Ottoman suzerain), contributed to the creation of modern Egypt, and Nubar Pasha, first minister to Ibrahim Pasha.

In the mid-nineteenth century, at a time when Egyptian power extended along the Red Sea as far as northern Eritrea, the Armenians of Alexandria and Cairo were in touch with Armenian colonies in Ethiopia, at Gondar and Addis Ababa.

THE ARMENIANS OF EGYPT

By the beginning of the twentieth century, there were Armenian communities in Paris, London, Vienna, Venice, Marseilles, Antwerp, and Lvov, in Romania and Bulgaria, at Djulfa (near Ispahan in Persia), Alexandria, Madras, Calcutta, Singapore, and Jakarta. Outside the Ottoman Empire, the Russian empire and Persia, the largest number of Armenians was in the United States—fifty to eighty thousand—principally in Boston, New York, Philadelphia, and California. Most of them arrived in the United States following the massacres of 1895–1896 under the Ottoman sultan Abdul-Hamid II. A small number went to Canada, especially Toronto and Montreal. In the Russian Empire, they were mostly at Baku and Tbilisi; in the Ottoman Empire at Constantinople, Smyrna, and Trebizond.

THE DIASPORA CIRCA 1900

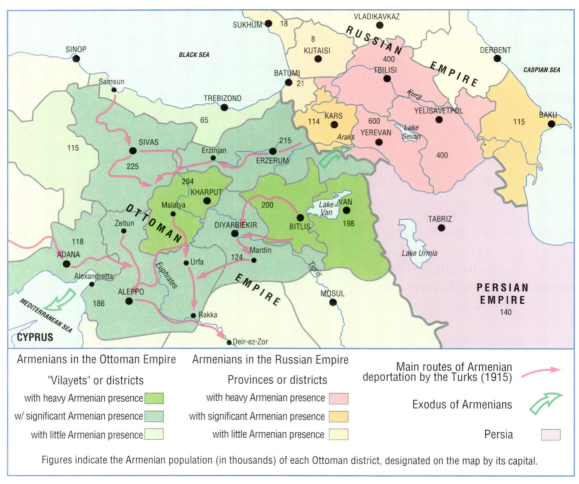

Armenians in the Ottoman Empire

"Vilayets" or districts

with heavy Armenian presence 🟩

w/ significant Armenian presence 🟩

with little Armenian presence 🟩

Armenians in the Russian Empire

Provinces or districts

with heavy Armenian presence 🟪

with significant Armenian presence 🟨

with little Armenian presence 🟨

Main routes of Armenian deportation by the Turks (1915) ➜

Exodus of Armenians ➜

Persia 🟪

Figures indicate the Armenian population (in thousands) of each Ottoman district, designated on the map by its capital.

▲ THE GENOCIDE

Until the appearance in the Ottoman Empire of modern nationalism, an idea spread by Europe, and of French socialist or Russian populist ideas—that is, until the last quarter of the nineteenth century—the Armenians enjoyed conditions deemed acceptable to the spirit of the age. Like the Greeks or the Jews, the Armenians enjoyed the rights of *millet,* that is, communal self-government granted to non-Muslims. While the Armenian peasantry lived in often very harsh conditions, a bourgeoisie of notables, merchants, bankers, and craftsmen had occupied enviable positions since the seventeenth century.

During the First World War the Ottoman Empire, which had pan-Turk ambitions, allied itself with the Central Powers (Germany and Austria-Hungary). In a climate clouded by reversals in the Caucasus, where they were fighting the Russians, the Young Turks, fearing that the Armenians, like the nationalists in the Balkans,[1] would seek independence under the leadership of their political organizations, decided to deport the Armenian population from the Russo-Turkish border.

In reality, it was the whole Armenian population of Anatolia as far as the Syrian border that was deported in 1915–1916. Different sources put the total number of Armenians in the Ottoman Empire at between 1.5 and 2 million. After the liquidation of the elite and notables of Constantinople and the summary execution of Armenian soldiers enrolled in the Ottoman army and then disarmed, general deportation led to large-scale massacres. This genocide led to the death of forty to fifty percent of the Armenian population,[2] according to divergent sources.

The genocide of 1915 eradicated the Armenians from Asia Minor and

THE GENOCIDE

1. All the Balkan countries liberated themselves between 1878 and 1912.

2. Which makes the number of dead between 600,000 (according to the historian Justin McCarthy, a recent champion of the Turkish viewpoint) and 1,100,000 (according to the pro-Armenian German pastor Johannes Lepsius).

especially the six vilayets (provinces) where most of them were concentrated. Following the Treaty of Lausanne (1923), a few tens of thousands of Armenians remained in Turkey, mostly in Istanbul.

The deportation—or flight—took three directions: the Armenians of the vilayet of Van mostly sought refuge in the Caucasus and Iran, as did some of the Armenians from northeastern Anatolia who had managed to escape deportation.

The bulk of the Armenian population of Anatolia was deported to the deserts of Syria and Mesopotamia. The survivors settled, sometimes provisionally, in Aleppo, Damascus, and Beirut, at the time of the French mandate. Some reached France or the United States.

The passports of Armenians leaving Constantinople in the 1920s were stamped "No return possible." The eviction of the Armenians from Turkey was almost total. Some of these political refugees obtained a Nansen passport (1924).[1]

In the industrialized countries, conditions were precarious, as they are for all who arrive with no capital but their labor power and no command of the language of the country.

Marseilles, the suburbs of Paris, the poor districts of New York or Buenos Aires were home to most of the first generation of survivors of the great massacres. In California, at Fresno, the Armenians became farm laborers, while some of the immigrants worked in factories.

1. Named after the Norwegian explorer and humanitarian, the League of Nations' first High Commissioner for Refugees.

In the Russian Empire, the last quarter of the nineteenth century saw the appearance of an Armenian bourgeoisie of merchants and industrialists, mainly at Baku but also in Tbilisi, Batum, the Caucasus, and, farther north, in Odessa, Rostov-on-Don, Moscow, and Saint Petersburg. General Loris-Melikoff, the victor over Ottoman troops in the Caucasus in the war of 1877 and later Alexander II's minister of the interior, came from this Armenian diaspora.

After the Revolution, an independent republic of Armenia was formed, which lasted from 1918 to 1920. It was incorporated into the Soviet Union in December 1920. In the meantime it had taken in some 300,000 refugees from Anatolia—out of a total population of 750,000.

All this suggests that, at the end of the First World War, the situation of most Armenians was indeed dramatic. Many were living in camps hastily thrown up on wasteland on the outskirts of Aleppo, Damascus, Beirut, and Athens (yet Greece took in about 1.2 million Greeks expelled from Asia Minor, exchanged after the Treaty of Lausanne for 650,000 Muslims who were expelled to Turkey), Plovdiv, and Sofia in Bulgaria, and in Cyprus.

SOVIET ARMENIA ▶

SOVIET ARMENIA

Armenia

Nagorno-Karabakh

Other Republics with significant Armenian minorities

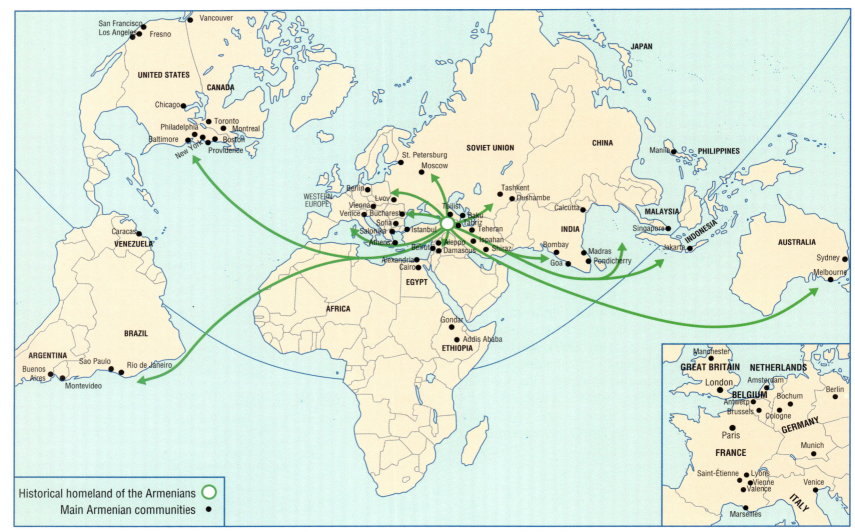

San Francisco
Los Angeles
Fresno
Vancouver

UNITED STATES
CANADA

Chicago

Philadelphia
Baltimore
New York
Providence
Toronto
Montreal
Boston

St. Petersburg
Moscow

SOVIET UNION

CHINA

JAPAN

Manila
PHILIPPINES

Berlin
Lvoy
WESTERN
EUROPE
Vienna
Venice
Bucharest
Sofia
Salonika
Istanbul
Athens
Tbilisi
Baku
Tabriz
Teheran
Tashkent
Dushambe

Calcutta

MALAYSIA

Singapore
INDONESIA

Beirut
Aleppo
Damascus
Ispahan
Shiraz
INDIA

Bombay

Madras
Pondicherry
Goa

Jakarta

AUSTRALIA

Sydney
Melbourne

Caracas
VENEZUELA

Alexandria
Cairo
EGYPT

AFRICA

Gondar
Addis Ababa
ETHIOPIA

BRAZIL

ARGENTINA
Buenos
Aires
Montevideo
Sao Paulo
Rio de Janeiro

Historical homeland of the Armenians
Main Armenian communities

Manchester
GREAT BRITAIN
NETHERLANDS
London
Amsterdam
BELGIUM
Antwerp
Brussels
Bochum
Cologne
Berlin
GERMANY

Paris
FRANCE
Munich

Saint-Étienne
Lyons
Vienne
Valence
Venice
ITALY

Marseilles

▲ THE ARMENIAN DIASPORA THROUGHOUT THE WORLD

The Armenian diaspora—some 1.8 million outside the former Soviet Union—is especially large today in North America. There are some 600,000 in the United States, almost half of them in California. In Canada there are almost 50,000. In the West as in the Middle East, communities of Armenian origin are strongly represented in the professions and the middle classes.

France, with which Armenians have traditionally had close historical and cultural links, is home to 250,000 Armenians, perhaps more, concentrated mainly in Paris, Lyons, and Marseilles.

Argentina (50,000?) and Australia (25,000) are also major diaspora centers.

Although numbers in the Middle East have been steadily declining with the rise of religious and national identity crises in the last two decades, there are still many Armenians there. More and more of the Armenian diaspora in Iran (100,000?), Syria (80,000?), and above all Lebanon (100,000) are migrating to Western countries. The diaspora's center of gravity, long centered in the Near East, has shifted to North America and France.

The Armenian diaspora in the former Soviet Union (outside the republic of Armenia) numbers some 1.5 million: 350,000 in Georgia, 800,000 in Russia, 100,000 in Azerbaijan (Upper Karabakh), 100,000 in central Asia, and 40,000 in Ukraine.

THE SITUATION TODAY

THE ARMENIAN CHURCH

The Armenian Apostolic Church—autonomous since the end of the fifth century—remains the symbol of the national personality. It is the only institution common to all Armenians, although it has a dual leadership. Syria, Lebanon, Iran, Greece, and Cyprus are attached to the Catholicos of Antilyas (Lebanon). The former U.S.S.R., Turkey, Europe, and America are in varying degrees under the Catholicos of Echmiadzin (Armenia). In principle, primacy belongs to the latter. Over 90 percent of Armenians belong to the Apostolic Church, sometimes called the Gregorian Church (after Saint Gregory the Illuminator). The rest are divided almost equally into Catholics and Protestants (Evangelical Church). There are many active local and transnational community organizations (schools, welfare associations, etc.) The Armenian-language press manages to survive (*Hairenik* in Boston, *Haratch* in Paris, *Aztak* in Beirut, etc.).

THE TRADITIONAL PARTIES

The political parties, although a hundred years old, have survived in the diaspora with a mixture of obstinacy in transmitting a national heritage and a conservatism almost untouched by the great changes brought about by modernity. The Dashnaks (social democrats) and the Ramgavars (liberals) both still have their followings and activists.

Securing international recognition of the genocide mobilized the energies of the diaspora in various forms. A very small minority resorted to publicity terrorism between 1975 and 1983 (Justice Commandos for the Armenian Genocide, close to the Dashnak party, and the third-worldist Armenian Secret Army for the Liberation of Armenia); but most engaged in legal activities: publishing books and documents; the Permanent Peoples' Tribunal (Paris, 1984); recognition after a long procedural struggle of the genocide by the U.N. Human Rights Subcommittee (Geneva, 1986); recognition of the genocide by the European Council (1987). The fight for official recognition by the democracies continues in the United States, where Turkey defends its viewpoint largely through the threat of reprisals against American interests. Official international recognition of the genocide of the Armenians has not yet occurred. Turkey continues to deny the crime.

We have no statistics on Armenia and the Armenians following the pogroms at Sumgait in 1988 and Baku in 1989 perpetrated by Azerbaijanis and clashes between Azeris and Armenians. But it is reasonable to estimate that some 250,000 Armenians left Azerbaijan (and notably Baku) between 1988 and 1990. For their part, about 200,000 Azerbaijanis have left Armenia, freely or otherwise.

The terrible earthquake of December 1988 and the exceptional international solidarity which was expressed at that time brought Armenia back to the center of the concerns of a diaspora which found in it a common cause and, for some, prospects for action beyond simply keeping faith with a past.

The political prospects and the democratic opening that have arisen from Gorbachev's *glasnost,* by helping to put an end to the hegemony of the

POLITICAL DEMANDS

Armenian Communist party, have radically altered the relationship between the diaspora and Armenia. The new democratically elected leadership—those who belonged to the Karabakh committee for the self-determination of the Armenian population—decided to demand all the attributes of sovereignty Gorbachev had laid out.

Ex-Soviet Armenia has thus taken on a more-than-symbolic reality for the diaspora.

Text by the American writer William Saroyan (1908–1981), who was born in Fresno, California, the son of Armenian immigrants.

"I should like to see any power of the world destroy this race, this small tribe of unimportant people, whose wars have all been fought and lost, whose structures have crumbled, literature is unread, music is unheard, and prayers are no more answered. Go ahead, destroy Armenia. See if you can do it. Send them into the desert without bread or water. Burn their homes and churches. Then see if they will not laugh, sing, and pray again. For when two of them meet anywhere in the world, see if they will not create a New Armenia."

1. Armenian church in Singapore (Photo © Le Priol-Frangulian). Two Armenian churches in ▶
California: 2. in Hollywood, 3. in Glendale (Photo © Kenneth Martin).

1

2

3

▲ Pilgrimage in Saintes-Maries-de-la-mer, important Gypsy assembly which takes place each year at the end of May (Photo © J. Koudelka-Magnum).

THE GYPSY DIASPORA

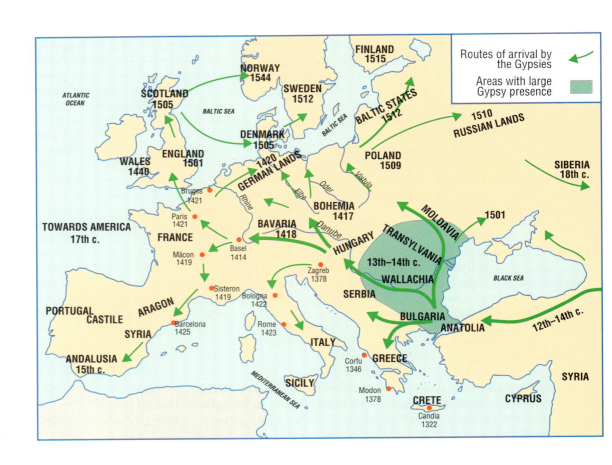

It is their very state of dispersion that makes Gypsies Gypsies. Without territory, without archives, they have doubtless been the sole nomads who have not been either hunters or herders. Originating in India, they lived in Persia in about the tenth century, and later in Anatolia.

Two texts appear to show evidence of the presence of Gypsies in Iran in about the tenth century: one by the historian Hamza of Ispahan and one by the poet Firdausi (ca. 930–1020) who, in his *Shah Nama* (Book of Kings), tells of the presence of a tribe of musicians (whom he calls Luri) sent by the ruler of India. This tribe, called "Zott" by Hamza of Ispahan, is said to have become nomadic after consuming the grain and cattle provided by the king of Persia.

At the beginning of the fourteenth century there is evidence of their presence in Europe: 1322 in Crete; 1346 on Corfu; 1348 in Serbia; 1370 in Wallachia and Transylvania; 1378 in Zagreb (Croatia); 1399 in Bohemia.

In the fifteenth century the number of written documents mentioning their passage increases. The main centers of dispersion at the time were Moldavia, Transylvania, Wallachia, and Hungary. In the beginning, the Gypsy groups often enjoyed privileges and protection granted by ecclesiastical or royal authorities. Thus at the beginning of the fifteenth century Sigismund, king of Hungary, Bohemia, Dalmatia, and other lands, issued letters of protection to a group of Gypsies. Later, in western Europe, it was these letters which caused the Gypsies to be called "Bohemians."

But this privileged situation did not last long. After a benevolent welcome mixed with astonishment at their way of life and appearance, hostility became very common.

At the beginning of the sixteenth century the passage of Gypsies is mentioned in northern Europe.

The Gypsies, who today describe themselves as Romanies, have been called by various names:

Tsiganes in French (from the Greek *Athinganoi* or *Atsinkanos*); *Zigeuner* in German; *Chinguene* in Turkish; *Tigani* in Romanian; *Ciganyok* in Hungarian; *Gitanos* (Egitanos) in Spanish, in reference to Egypt, from where they are said to have come; Gypsies in English; *Farao Nepek* in Hungarian; *Ejiftos* in Greek; *Bohemians* because they came from Bohemia carrying letters of commendation from the rulers of Bohemia; *Romanischals; Manus; Suntis* (from Piedmont); *Romanies*, finally, for those who claim that they came from the area along the Danube in southeastern Europe, etc.

◄ "Bohemians" at the turn of the century (Photo © Roger-Viollet).

Just as settled people remain settled people even when they travel, so the Gypsy is a nomad even when not traveling. A Gypsy at rest remains a traveler. So it is really more accurate to speak of sedentarized Gypsies rather than sedentary Gypsies, for the former suggests a temporary condition for people who still consider movement meaningful and vital. . . .

As an element of identity, being "Travelers" lets the Gypsies mark themselves off from those who aren't, the gadze, *the non-Gypsies, the peasants, the sedentary. . . . Travelers move on. Their living space is experience itself, never a shut or bounded territory, but a flexible identity unattached to any particular piece of earth: the land of the Gypsies lies within themselves. . . .*

The present contains both the past gone by and the future, which will be here soon enough—it need not be imagined. The present is so important that you can both forget and not bother to look ahead, leave things behind by shifting the problems created by others, bend to arbitrary obligations without breaking. This notion of time and space provides a flexibility and adaptability that have enabled Gypsy populations to live for centuries scattered among hostile peoples, meanwhile developing the features of a special culture of their own.

THE "TRAVELER"

in J.-P. Liégeois, Gypsies, An Illustrated History, *trans. Tony Berrett (London: Al Saqi Books, 1986).*

TRADES   The Gypsy tribes that originated especially in southeastern Europe (Romanies) distinguish themselves from one another by the names of trades:

Kalderas: pot makers

Churara: sieve makers

Lovara: horse dealers

Lautari: musicians, lute players, etc.

The trades practiced by Gypsies are compatible with nomadism and leave people free to arrange their own work schedule: smithing, metalworking (Hungary), tinning, gold washing (Romania, Bosnia), chair mending, basket making, bricklaying, brick making, coach driving (Moldavia, Wallachia), chimney sweeping, horse dealing, regrinding, seasonal farm labor. Today they work as second-hand car dealers, scrap merchants, mechanics, second-hand dealers, in circus trades, fairs and music, with two main centers: eastern Europe (ex-Yugoslavia, Hungary, Romania, Bulgaria, and Russia) and Spain, where the Gitanos have made a considerable contribution to flamenco—*cante jondo*—and bullfighting. Women are fortunetellers.

REJECTION   Opposition to the *gadzo* (the non-Gypsy) and rejection by him of the Gypsy and his way of life have defined the odd position of the Gypsy; the two worlds see one another as antagonistic. In Europe, where, thanks to state archives, we are less poorly informed about their history from the fifteenth century down to the Nazi genocide, relations have almost always been tinged with hostility.

Rejection or forced assimilation were the two policies generally followed throughout Europe, before the attempt at liquidation in the Nazi period.

Perceived as ne'er-do-wells and troublemakers, the Gypsies were banished from almost every country: France, Germany, the Netherlands, Switzerland, etc. Gypsy hunts were organized with a bounty on their capture.

They were forbidden to stay, forbidden to travel, forbidden to move about in groups of more than three or four. People could be punished for taking them in, or giving them alms, while "Bohemians" in the sixteenth and seventeenth centuries were usually sent to the galleys on the least pretext. As vagrants they were suspected of kidnapping children and accused of witchcraft.

In France, legislation prohibited "Bohemians" (vagabonds and vagrants) from staying in the country, condemned them to banishment; if they were caught a second time, they were sent to the galleys through a series of judicial decisions between 1504 and 1803.

In Romania, the Gypsies were reduced to outright slavery in the fourteenth century. Apart from putting them to death, a master had every right over them. The lords and clergy had numerous Gypsy slaves. Gypsy slavery in Romania was abolished only in 1856.

"By the sons and heirs of Serdar Nicolai Nica of Bucharest, for sale: 200 Gypsy families. The men are mainly locksmiths, goldsmiths, boot makers, musicians, and peasants. Not less than five familes per lot. Easy terms."

"FOR SALE"

Advertisement in the newspaper Luna *(Agram) in 1845* *(in J.-P. Liégeois,* Gypsies*).*

Spanish Legislation on Gypsies[1]		
Year	Order	Punishment
1499	Find a trade and master, cease traveling together, within 60 days.	100 lashes and banishment. For repeat offenders: amputation of ears, 60 days in chains, and banishment. Third-time offenders to become slaves of those who capture them.
1560 and after	Traveling in groups of more than 2 forbidden. "Dress and clothing of Gitanos" banned.	Up to 18 years in the galleys, for those over 14. Repetition: for nomads, death; for settled people, the galleys.
1619	Banishment of all Gitanos from the kingdom within 6 months or settlement in a locality with over 1,000 inhabitants. Dress, name and language of the Gitanos banned.	Death.
1695	Census of all Gypsies within 30 days; then 30 more days to leave the kingdom or settle in a locality of over 200 inhabitants. Work on the land (compulsory). Horses forbidden. Fairs and markets forbidden.	Men: 6 years in the galleys. Women: 100 lashes and banishment. For repeat offenders, 8 years in the galleys for men, 200 lashes and banishment for women.
1745	Settlement in assigned places within two weeks.	Execution: "It is legal to fire upon them and to take their life." Churches no longer asylums.

1. Adapted from J.-P. Liégeois, *Gypsies*.

| 1749 | Great roundup and various decrees. Separation of "the bad and the good" through inquiries and witnesses' reports. | For the "bad," public works; escapees to be hanged. Motherless girls sent to poorhouses or into service for honest people. |
| 1783 | Reiteration of previous orders: dress, way of life, and language forbidden, settlement compulsory, all within 90 days. | Branding. For repeat offenders: "death with no appeal." |

Discriminatory measures were only abolished after the end of the Franco regime.

"Census-taking in a temporary camp of Bohemians ▲ in France." The caravan is emblematic of the Gypsies' nomadic lifestyle; save for these forerunners of today's trailer or mobile home and the presence of large numbers of tamed animals, the boundaries of the camp would not have otherwise been delineated. Illustrated supplement to the *Petit Journal*, 5 May 1895 (Photo C. J. Vigne).

RELIGION AND TRADITIONS

Gypsies have adopted the religion of the countries in which they reside: they are Catholics in Spain, Protestants in northern Europe, Orthodox in Romania and Russia, Muslims in Turkey. Language, on the other hand, with its various dialects, remains one of the marks of Gypsy identity. The family cell is solid and the father wields authority. Marriages outside the community are the exception. The men generally dress according to the norms of the country where they are living, whereas women dress traditionally in long multicolored skirts.

THE GYPSIES IN EUROPE

1449: In Germany, Gypsies driven out of Frankfurt-am-Main.

1500: At the request of Emperor Maximilian I, the Augsburg Reichstag adopts a law expelling Gypsies from the Holy Roman Empire.

1530, 1554, 1562: In England, laws are enacted that give Gypsies the choice of taking up a trade or being expelled.

1546: In England, they are forced on board ships and expelled to Calais (then under English rule).

Bohemia and Slovakia welcome the Gypsies in the fifteenth and sixteenth centuries. They can stay freely in Prague. The influx of Gypsies from countries where they are persecuted changes this initial attitude.

1579: Gypsies expelled from Saxony.

1648: Following the Thirty Years War, a new decree provides the death penalty for any Gypsies taken on the territory of Saxony.

1710: Frederick I of Prussia issues a decree condemning men to forced labor, women to branding, and children to be taken away from their parents.

1710: Joseph I orders all adult males to be hanged and boys and women mutilated: the left ear cut off in Bohemia, the right ear in Moravia.

1721 and 1726: Similar edicts are repeated. Whole groups are hanged or slaughtered.

1721: Emperor Charles VI orders the extermination of the Gypsies.

1725: Frederick William I condemns any adult Gypsy, man or woman, caught in Prussian territory to be hanged.

In the second half of the eighteenth century a new policy emerges, both in the Austrian Empire under Maria Theresa and Joseph II, and in Prussia under Frederick II.

In the context of the Enlightenment and benevolent despotism, attempts are made to settle and assimilate the Gypsies. In the Hapsburg empire, where they are particularly numerous, Maria Theresa decrees that they must settle (1758), while Joseph II makes it compulsory for Gypsy children to attend school and bans Gypsy language, clothing, and music.

The American continent has seen various waves of Gypsy immigration. In the seventeenth century deportation measures enacted by the Portuguese and Spanish authorities led Gypsies to Brazil and Argentina.

Emigration to the United States dates from the second half of the nineteenth century, with the waves of migrants who left Russia and Romania or the Austro-Hungarian Empire after 1880.

THE GYPSIES IN THE UNITED STATES

THE NAZI PERSECUTIONS

In 1938, the Nazis issued an edict concerning "the Gypsy threat." On 1 March 1943, all the Gypsies in Germany (about 22,000) were arrested and deported to Poland, most of them to Auschwitz. Twenty thousand died there. It is estimated that between 250,000 (Liégeois) and 400,000 (C. Tyrnauer[1]) Gypsies were exterminated between 1943 and 1945.

NUREMBERG

Text of judgment pronounced by the American judge at the 8 April 1948 session of the Nuremberg tribunal.

The "Einsatzgruppen" were also ordered to shoot the Gypsies. No explanation was given why this inoffensive people who, over the centuries, has given its share of wealth in music and song should be hunted down like wild game. Picturesque in dress and customs, they have amused and entertained society, and sometimes annoyed it by their indolence. But nobody condemned them as a mortal threat to organized society, that is, nobody except National Socialism which, by the voice of Hitler, Himmler and Heydrich, ordered their liquidation.

GYPSIES IN THE COMMUNIST COUNTRIES

In the U.S.S.R., after a period in the 1920s when the Gypsies were recognized as a nationality, their cultural specificity was soon denied by Stalin, who dissolved the "Union of all the Gypsies of Russia."

While sedentarization was generally effective, integration failed.

Under Communist rule, the Gypsies were not considered a minority and thus had no rights as such—the Gypsy problem being treated as a "social problem."

In the Communist-ruled countries of central and southeastern Europe following the Second World War, nomadism was strictly forbidden. The policy pursued aimed at sedentarization, schooling, and assimilation, the means

1. C. Tyrnauer, *Gypsies and the Holocaust: A Bibliography and Introductory Essay* (Montreal: Concordia University, 1989).

deployed being dispersion and/or deportation. No "Socialist" country ever recognized the Gypsies as an ethnic or linguistic minority. The most active de facto discrimination occurred in Romania.

Since the beginning of the twentieth century there has been a steady shift westward of the Gypsy population of southeastern Europe. This movement has speeded up in the last twenty years with the exodus of Gypsies from Yugoslavia. More recently, there has been an exodus of Gypsies from Romania by way of Czechoslovakia heading mostly for the European Community countries. In France, for example, there have recently developed concentrations of Gypsies from Romania in Nanterre, Metz, and Rouen.

Gypsies in Czechoslovakia, 1965 (Photo © J. Koudelka-Magnum) ▲

FINLAND

NORWAY

SWEDEN

Baltic States

NORTH SEA

IRELAND

Manchester

DENMARK

Hamburg

UNITED KINGDOM

London

NETHERLANDS

Amsterdam

Antwerp

GERMANY

Ruhr

BELGIUM

Cologne

Paris

Frankfurt

Rhine

CZECHOSLOVAKIA

Bohemia

FRANCE

Loire

Munich

Danube

Vistula

Elbe

POLAND

Galicia

SOVIET UNION

Ukraine

Dnieper

Bessarabia

Slovakia

Moldavia

SWITZERLAND

Lyons

AUSTRIA

HUNGARY

Croatia

Transylvania

ROMANIA

Milan

Marseilles

Genoa

ITALY

Serbia

Wallachia

BLACK SEA

PORTUGAL

SPAIN

Barcelona

Corsica

Rome

YUGOSLAVIA

Macedonia

BULGARIA

Istanbul

Sardinia

ALBANIA

TURKEY

ANDALUSIA

GREECE

Cyprus

MEDITERRANEAN

Sicily

Crete

SEA

▲ GYPSY DISPLACEMENTS THROUGHOUT EUROPE

It is exceedingly difficult to make a reasonable estimate of the number of Gypsies in the world. Most states in which they live provide no statistics about them. The number of Gypsies in Turkey, for example, is quite un-known.

THE SITUATION TODAY

Their total population is probably between eight and fifteen million (the widest variation given by some experts).

Some estimates

	Conservative	High
Ex-Yugoslavia	700,000	1,000,000
Romania	500,000	1,500,000
Hungary	400,000	800,000
Ex-Czechoslovakia	300,000	500,000
Poland	30,000	80,000
Ex-Soviet Union	300,000	1,000,000
Bulgaria	300,000	500,000
Spain	500,000	1,000,000
France	250,000	300,000
Italy	70,000	100,000
Germany	100,000	120,000
Great Britain	70,000	100,000
Greece	100,000	120,000
United States	100,000	150,000
Other countries	250,000	500,000

THE ROMANY UNION

During the 1960s and '70s, in western Europe, in Yugoslavia, and in Greece, the Gypsies began to organize. Legislation affecting them was gradually modified.

In 1971 the First World Romany Congress was held in London. Delegates from fourteen countries took part, in addition to observers from other countries. The delegates unanimously rejected the names Gypsy, Tsigane, or Gitano and adopted the name Romany. A Second World Congress was held in Geneva in 1978, this time with delegates from twenty-six countries. The Romanies stressed their attachment to the "mother country," India. India had been supporting Gypsy demands at the United Nations since 1972. The Romanies' aim was to secure recognition by international bodies, obtain the status of a minority in the Eastern bloc countries, fight against policies of rejection and assimilation, work to standardize their language, and pursue claims for war reparations from Germany.

In its resolution of 31 August 1977, the Commission on Human Rights of the Economic and Social Council, the Subcommittee on Prevention of Discrimination and Protection of Minorities of the United Nations, called on "countries which have Gypsies (Romanies) within their borders to grant such people, if they have not already done so, all the rights enjoyed by the rest of the population."

In 1979, the U.N. gave consultative status to the "Romany Union" representing seventy-one associations in twenty-one countries.

The Third World Congress was held in Gottingen in 1981. There were three hundred delegates representing twenty-two states: eighteen in Europe, including, for the first time, four from Eastern Europe (Bulgaria, Hungary, Romania, and Poland), plus the United States, Australia, India, and Pakistan.

Gypsies in Spain: the "Gitanos" (Photo J. Koudelka-Magnum). ▲

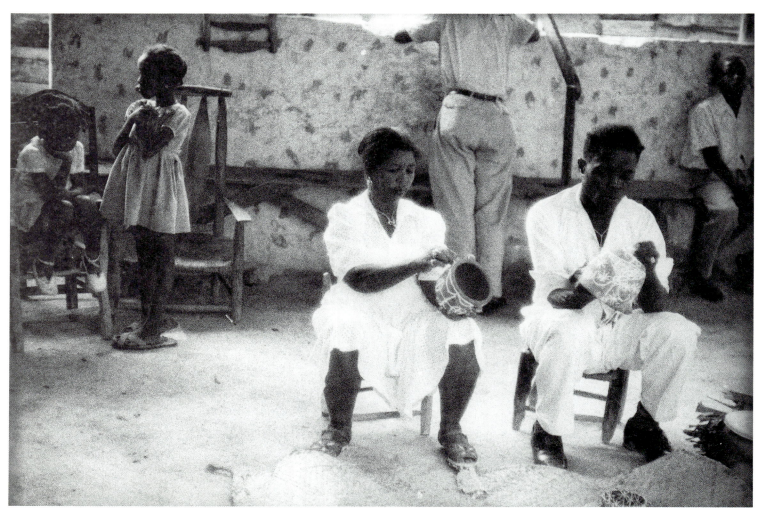

▲ Voodoo in Haiti (Photo © Arnold-Magnum).

THE BLACK DIASPORA

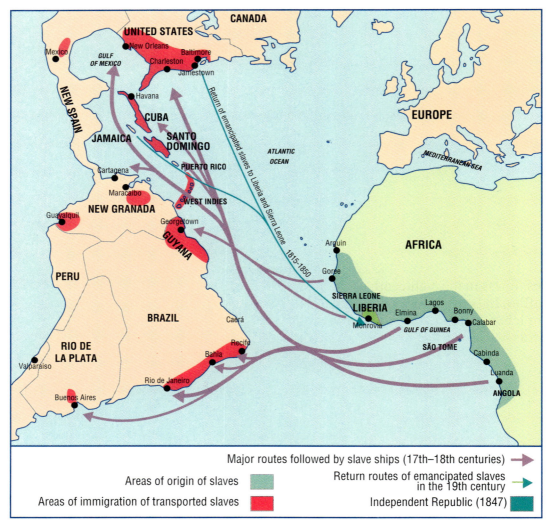

CANADA

UNITED STATES

Mexico

GULF
OF MEXICO

New Orleans
Baltimore
Charleston
Jamestown

Havana

CUBA

SANTO
DOMINGO

JAMAICA

NEW SPAIN

PUERTO RICO

Cartagena

Maracaibo

Guayaquil

NEW GRANADA

WEST INDIES

Georgetown

GUYANA

PERU

BRAZIL

Caerá

RIO DE
LA PLATA

Recife

Bahia

Valparaiso

Rio de Janeiro

Buenos Aires

EUROPE

ATLANTIC
OCEAN

MEDITERRANEAN SEA

Return of emancipated slaves to Liberia and Sierra Leone 1815-1850

Arguin

Goree

AFRICA

SIERRA LEONE

LIBERIA

Monrovia

Elmina

Lagos

Bonny

Calabar

GULF OF GUINEA

SÃO TOME

Cabinda

Luanda

ANGOLA

Major routes followed by slave ships (17th–18th centuries)

Areas of origin of slaves

Areas of immigration of transported slaves

Return routes of emancipated slaves
in the 19th century

Independent Republic (1847)

▲ THE SLAVE TRADE

From the mid-sixteenth to the mid-nineteenth centuries, the slave trade was carried on first by the Portuguese and Spaniards and then by the Dutch, English, and French.

In three centuries this seaborne traffic in slaves scattered some ten to twelve million blacks across the New World.

The slave trade involved both Bantu and non-Bantu populations and affected Africa from Dakar to Luanda—not to mention a slave trade (on a far smaller scale) out of Mozambique.

The slaves were initially used in the sugar cane plantations in Brazil and the West Indies. It was in the eighteenth century that the slave trade became a large-scale affair. In Brazil, the development of coffee-growing increased the demand for labor. In 1817, out of a total population of 3.8 million there were 2.5 million blacks. In the southern United States slavery also grew enormously in the eighteenth century (Virginia, Maryland, North and South Carolina).[1] This movement intensified at the beginning of the nineteenth century with the spread of cotton-growing and weaving industries. But the bulk of slaves in the eighteenth century arrived in the slave markets of the Caribbean: the West Indies, coastal Colombia and Venezuela, the Guianas.

The second market after the Caribbean was Brazil.

In the first quarter of the nineteenth century, about 1810 to 1820, the size of the African-American population, slave or free, was estimated at 2 to 2.5 million for the United States, 2.5 to 3 million for the Caribbean, and about 2.5 million for Brazil. Except for Cuba, where they amount to almost 30 percent of the total population, and Puerto Rico, where they amount to

AFRICANS IN THE AMERICAS

1. On the history of black America, see Lerone Bennett, Jr., *Before the Mayflower,* rev. ed. (New York: Penguin Books, 1993).

over one-third, the black or mulatto population today make up the vast majority in the West Indies (65 to 70 percent). In Haiti the population is wholly of African origin. In Surinam and Guiana the black or mulatto population varies between one-third and 40 percent. About 15 percent of the populations of Columbia and Venezuela are of African origin and are concentrated on the Caribbean coast.

In Brazil blacks and mulattos make up almost half the total population—sixty-five to seventy million. In the United States blacks represent 12 percent of the total population. (The category of mulatto does not exist in the United States: a black is a black, however light the color of his skin.)

It can be estimated that today there are over 120 million people of African origin on the American continent.

"The slave-ships carried not only men, women and children, but their gods, beliefs, and traditional folklore."[2] Vivid traces of these cultural traits still exist and have developed, sometimes through syncretism, particularly in the West Indies and Brazil: voodoo in Haiti, traces of which can be found in Cuba; *batuque* in Puerto Rico; *caboclo candomblé* in the Bahia-Pernambuco region.

In the United States, on the other hand, ancestral religions have tended to disappear, and reformed Christianity has exercised a considerable influence.

2. R Bastide, *Les Ameriques noires* (Paris: Payot, 1967); C. Hurst, *African Civilisations in the New World,* trans. by Peter Green (London: 1971).

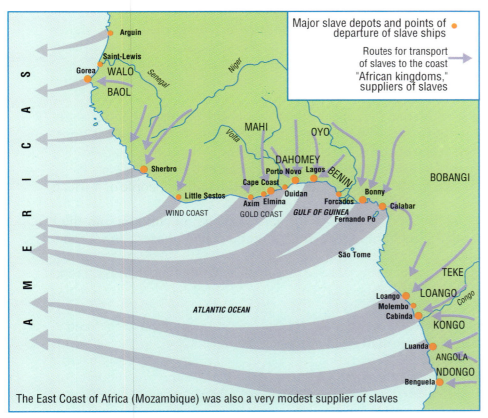

Major slave depots and points of ● departure of slave ships

Routes for transport of slaves to the coast ➜

"African kingdoms," suppliers of slaves

Arguin

Saint-Lewis

Gorea

WALO

BAOL

Senegal

Niger

MAHI

OYO

Volta

DAHOMEY

Porto Novo   Lagos

BENIN

Cape Coast   Ouidan

Sherbro

Little Sestos

Axim Elmina

WIND COAST

GOLD COAST

Forcados

Bonny

Calabar

Fernando Po

GULF OF GUINEA

BOBANGI

São Tome

TEKE

Loango   LOANGO

Molembo   Congo

Cabinda

KONGO

ATLANTIC OCEAN

Luanda

ANGOLA

NDONGO

Benguela

A M E R I C A S

The East Coast of Africa (Mozambique) was also a very modest supplier of slaves

PRINCIPAL ZONES OF ORIGIN OF THE SLAVES ▲

TOUSSAINT L'OUVERTURE (1743-1803), hero of Haiti's in- ▲ dependence and black liberation. Haiti was the first black independent republic (Photo Archives Tallandier).

ROOTS

From the creation of Liberia at the beginning of the nineteenth century to the West Indian Marcus Garvey's "Back to Africa" movement in the United States a century later and beyond, Africa has fueled aspirations for a return to their roots among a section of the elites in a more or less messianic way. This is the case, for example, with the Rastafarians, for whom the emperor of Abyssinia represented the messiah.

Flight or revolt had been the response to slavery. Exaltation of negritude, the third-worldism preached by the works of Frantz Fanon, Islam as compensation or rejection, or withdrawal into ethnicity have been some of the responses of blacks not economically integrated into industrial society, especially in the United States over the last three decades.

Even when blacks move from the countryside to the cities, in Brazil, for example, and more particularly in the United States (where since the First World War there has been a large-scale migration and urbanization of black communities), cultural traits survive creatively within black communities: for example, the samba schools in Rio, or jazz and other musical forms created by black Americans.

BLACKS IN THE UNITED STATES

In the United States, blacks are the largest minority, but the one whose economic and social integration is least assured.

On the eve of the Declaration of Independence, there were some half a million blacks in New England, almost 12 percent of the total population, almost all slaves. By 1787 the North had virtually accepted the abolition of slavery. The first internal American migration, to the North, occurred in the late nineteenth century. But in 1910, of the ten million blacks, nine million still lived in the South.

The First Jubilee Singers, a group of American Negro spiritual singers at the end of the nineteenth century, ▲ symbol of a crossed culture which was to give birth to jazz (Photo D.I.T.E.).

Black Americans today ▶

There have been numerous black revolts in the New World:

Haiti:
    1522, 1691, 1791.

Santo Domingo:
    1523, 1537, 1548.

British West Indies:
    1649, 1674, 1622, 1702, 1733, 1759.

13 colonies:
    several between 1663 and 1740.

United States:
    many between 1800 and 1864.

Puerto Rico:
    1811, 1822, 1823, 1833.

Jamaica:
    1831–1832.

Brazil (northeast):
    1807, 1809, 1813, 1826, 1827, 1828, 1830.

With the exception of Toussaint L'Ouverture's 1791 Haitian revolt, all of these struggles ended in failure.

Between 1910 and 1920 there was a great migration which took 300,000 blacks to the North and the Middle West. Large black communities came into being in cities such as New York, Philadelphia, and Chicago. After the Great Depression began in 1929 this movement accelerated.

Racial discrimination remained very prevalent until after the war. In 1954 the Supreme Court outlawed segregation in schools. Between 1954 and 1964 there was a bitterly fought struggle for civil rights, which were finally granted under President Johnson.

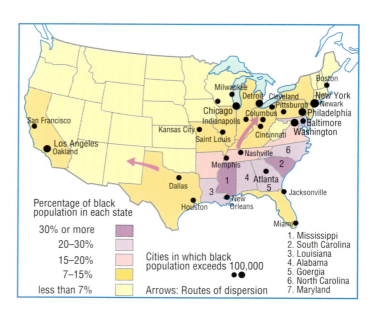

Percentage of black population in each state

30% or more
20–30%
15–20%
7–15%
less than 7%

Cities in which black population exceeds 100,000

Arrows: Routes of dispersion

1. Mississippi
2. South Carolina
3. Louisiana
4. Alabama
5. Goergia
6. North Carolina
7. Maryland

The United States: from slavery to equal rights

1619	Introduction of black slavery in Virginia.
1641	Massachusetts becomes first colony to give slavery statutory recognition.
1663	First slave insurrection in Virginia.
1688	First protest against slavery, by Quakers in Germantown (Pennsylvania).
1708	Slave revolt on Long Island (New York).
1712	Slave insurrection in New York City.
1739	Three slave uprisings in South Carolina.
1775	First abolitionist society created, in Philadelphia.
1776	United States Declaration of Independence. Enlistment of free blacks approved by Continental Congress.
1777	Slavery is abolished in Vermont.
1783	Six states in the North abolish slavery.
1787	Slavery excluded from Northwest Territory by Continental Congress.
1793	Fugitive Slave Act.
1800	Gabriel Prosser's revolt in Virginia.
1808	Ban on slave trade put into effect.
1811	Slave revolt in Louisiana.
1820	Start of "Return to Africa" movement: 20,000 blacks will eventually leave the U.S. for Liberia.
1830	Creation of the National Negro Convention Movement to fight slavery.
1831	Nat Turner's revolt in Virginia.
1839	Anti-slavery Liberty Party organized in New York.
1854	Kansas-Nebraska Act opens new territories to slavery.
1859	John Brown's raid on Harper's Ferry (Virginia).
1861–65	American Civil War.
1863	Lincoln's Emancipation Proclamation.
1867	First national meeting of the Ku Klux Klan, in Tennessee.
1870	Ratification of Fifteenth Amendment gives blacks right to vote.
1875	Civil Rights Bill outlaws discrimination in public places.
1881	Tennessee begins modern segregation practices, known as Jim Crow, and is followed by most southern states.

1883	Supreme Court declares Civil Rights Bill unconstitutional.
1885–96	Over a thousand blacks reported lynched.
1898	National Afro-American Council founded.
1903	W. E. B. Du Bois publishes *The Souls of Black Folk*.
1909	Establishment of the NAACP.
1914	Marcus Garvey founds the Universal Negro Improvement Association.
1915	Beginning of great black migration to the North.
1919	Race riots throughout the summer.
1927	Marcus Garvey is deported.
1930	Black Muslims founded.
1941	Franklin Roosevelt sets up the Fair Employment Practices Committee.
1943	Race riots in several cities.
1946	Congress declines to establish a permanent Fair Employment Practices Committee.
1947	Segregation ended in the military.
1948	California Supreme Court voids state statute banning interracial marriages.
1953	Racial segregation banned by Supreme Court in Washington, D.C., restaurants.

1954	Supreme Court orders school desegregation.
1955	Bus boycott in Montgomery, Alabama; Martin Luther King Jr. elected president of boycott organization.
1957	School desegregation in Little Rock, Arkansas.
1961	Freedom Riders attacked in Alabama.
1963	250,000 take part in March on Washington.
1964	Civil rights bill promising public accommodation and fair employment.
1965	Assassination of Malcolm X.
	Watts race riots (Los Angeles)
1966	Black Panthers founded.
1967	Thurgood Marshall named first black Supreme Court justice.
1968	Assassination of Martin Luther King Jr.
1970	Twelve blacks elected to Congress.
1980	Major race riot in Miami, Florida, as well as numerous Klan-related incidents throughout the South.
1987	Lt. Gen. Colin Powell named national security adviser.
1992	Riots in Los Angeles following beating of Rodney King by white policemen.

THE CHINESE DIASPORA

▲ Belleville district, Paris (France), one of the districts where the Asian diasporas have settled (Photo © P. Sachmann-Magnum).

The first significant migration of the Chinese dates from the thirteenth century, after the conquest of China by the Mongols in 1276. Some Chinese took refuge in Japan, Cambodia, and Vietnam. But the Mongol Yüan dynasty (1277–1367), far from being insulated, was interested in trade and exchanges; they developed ports and sent embassies to Cambodia, India, and Java. By the end of the Yüan dynasty in the fourteenth century, Chinese trading colonies were established in Cambodia, Java, Sumatra, and Singapore. Southeast Asia is thus a traditional area where Chinese have always migrated.

THE MONGOLS

When, under the Ming dynasty (1368–1644), Admiral Cheng Ho undertook his great maritime expeditions to the west as far as the east coast of Africa, between 1405 and 1433, the fleets encountered Chinese colonies in Thailand, Java, and Sumatra on the way.

At the beginning of the sixteenth century, even before the arrival of the Spaniards, the chronicles mention the presence of a large Chinese colony in the Philippines. This community was several times heavily persecuted. Anti-Chinese massacres took place in 1603 and 1639 during the Spanish occupation.

The sultans of Brunei encouraged Chinese immigration in the fifteenth and sixteenth centuries. The Chinese developed pepper growing there. Most left the country in the eighteenth century, after local persecution.

After the conquest of China by the Manchus, who established the Ch'ing dynasty (1644–1911), some Chinese left the country and took refuge in Taiwan, where there had been a Chinese colony since the Sung dynasty (960–1279).

THE MANCHUS

Others went to various countries in southeast Asia, where they formed secret societies that were anti-Manchu resistance movements. The Manchus prohibited all emigration. However, it continued clandestinely.

THE PENETRATION OF THE WEST

After defeat in the Opium War (1840–1842), China opened its doors to British trade, through Canton, Amoy, Shanghai, etc. These events led many Chinese to emigrate.

Between 1845 and 1900, 400,000 Chinese are estimated to have gone to the United States, Canada, Australia, and New Zealand. Not all stayed there. The exclusion policy of first Australia and then the United States led to some immigrants leaving their host country. But permanent Chinese colonies were established, especially in the United States and Canada.

Over the same period, some 1.5 million Chinese emigrated—almost all permanently—to southeast Asia (Indonesia, Thailand, Vietnam, Malaysia, Singapore). They worked in the mines (tin mines in Malaya and southern Siam) or as farm laborers.

Between 1842 and 1900 about 400,000 Chinese went to the West Indies and Latin America, mainly Peru (after 1848), Cuba (after 1847), and Chile.

All told, 2,300,000 Chinese went abroad between 1842 and 1900. Almost all came from southeastern China, which had been heavily hit by wars, epidemics, and famines.

Emigration involved a contract including reimbursement of the cost of the ticket by the worker. This system was introduced by the Europeans to deal with the labor problems resulting from the abolition of slavery. These immigrants went to the West Indies, the United States (during the gold rush),

Australia, or the countries of southeast Asia colonized by Europeans. Alongside the contract system there were also free workers or workers who had borrowed from their family or friends.

After 1859 the British established emigration centers in Canton with the cooperation of the Chinese authorities.

An article in the treaty signed in Beijing in 1860 between China and Great Britain legalized free emigration. In the same year France signed a similar treaty with China.

Spain followed in 1864. A convention on emigration was put into effect in 1866. Over the years that followed, China signed treaties on emigration with a number of countries: Peru (1868 and 1874), the United States (1880 and 1914), and Spain again (1877).

In fact the security of Chinese emigrants, whether volunteers or not, was not assured—signatures on contracts were often extorted.

It was only in 1899 that a decree was issued by the emperor of China to make Chinese ambassadors and consuls provide aid and support to citizens from their country.

Arrivals of Chinese labor in the nineteenth century[1] (1850–1910)

United States	200,000
Hawaii	30,000
Canada	35,000
Australia	73,000
New Zealand	5,000
Cuba*	150,000
Peru**	120,000
West Indies & Guiana	65,000
Total	678,000

The rest of the emigrants went to southeast Asia (including Hong Kong, Macao, and Taiwan) and by 1904 numbered some 7 million people.

All these figures, especially those for the Anglo-Saxon countries, fell after 1900 (and sometimes after 1885).

*Many Chinese left Cuba at the beginning of the twentieth century, others after 1960. In 1887 the number of Chinese was 45,000. By 1917 it was only 11,217 (*Statesman's Yearbook*, 1921).

**Chinese have left Peru en masse.

1. H. F. MacNair, *The Chinese Abroad* (Shanghai, 1924).

THE TERMS OF THE CONTRACT

In Australia in 1851:[1]

Duration	5 years	
Monthly wage	3 dollars	
Monthly deduction to reimburse cost of fare	0.5 dollars	
Monthly rations	sugar	1 lb.
	rice	10 lbs.
	meat	8 lbs.
	tea	2 oz.

Nature of work: shepherd, farmer, servant, farm laborer.

1. J. P. Simpson, *Twenty One Original Contracts Signed by J. P. Simpson, Contractor, and Chinese Laborers* (Sydney: Mitchell Library 1851).

In Cuba, the terms of the contract were for eight years at three dollars per month; eight years were stipulated in Martinique too. All sorts of methods, often illegal, including even kidnapping, were used to recruit people.

Transport was organized either by ship captains or by emigration agents or local agents (mainly Europeans). There was no shortage of abuses, often committed by local agents who would sell a cargo of emigrants to speculators in Cuba or Peru. In fact, almost all the Chinese workers arriving in Cuba and Peru were sold at auction.

Conditions on the crossing were terrible: the rate of mortality was between 12 and 25 percent. The highest losses occurred on ships bound for Peru and Cuba. Numerous cases of mutiny were recorded.

The most important thing for the migrant worker once he or she had arrived was to be able to put some money aside to reimburse the cost of the journey. Between 1856 and 1865 the cost of a passage from Hong Kong to San Francisco was one hundred dollars, from Macao to Peru seventy dollars, and from Canton to Australia sixty-six dollars.

The profit that speculators made on each migrant worker was in the region of 233–243 dollars.[1]

The passage to Australia took sixty to eighty-five days. To California and Peru via Yokohama and Hawaii it took 70 to 120 days, and to the West Indies around the Cape of Good Hope, 147 to 168 days.

It is estimated that 2,350,000 Chinese emigrants embarked at Chinese ports between 1840 and 1900. The number of those reaching their destination, given the percentage of deaths on the way, was between 1.8 and 2.1 million.

Free emigrants did not need a contract, since they paid their own passage in full.

1. Consul D. B. Robertson to Mr. Hammond, 9 June 1866, Cres. Resp., *The Engagement of Chinese Emigrants by British and French Subjects 1865–69* (G.B.F.O. Confidential Print n. 1737).

Famines and other disasters in China

1849	15 million deaths due to famine and epidemics.
1857	8 million deaths from famine.
1850–1864	The Taiping Rebellion and its repression leave 20 million dead.
1876–1878	10 million deaths from famine.

The Chinese population of southeast Asia[1] (1888)

Malayan peninsula	390,000
Singapore and Straits	200,000
Indochina	200,000
Siam (Thailand)[2]	1,000,000(?)
Burma	20,000
Dutch East Indies (Indonesia)[3]	350,000
Philippines	50,000

1. E. H. Parker, *Report on the Chinese Question,* 1888, G.B.F.O., Confidential Print n. 6039 X.

2. In Thailand today the Chinese account for 10 percent of the population. Entry into Siam was unrestricted. Forced labor did not exist. Unlike in other southeast Asian countries, intermarriage was common. The Chinese rapidly entered well-paying jobs and are very well integrated.

3. According to Dutch authorities, in 1917 there were 700,000 Chinese, 300,000 of them in Java, the rest on the east coast of Sumatra and in Borneo.

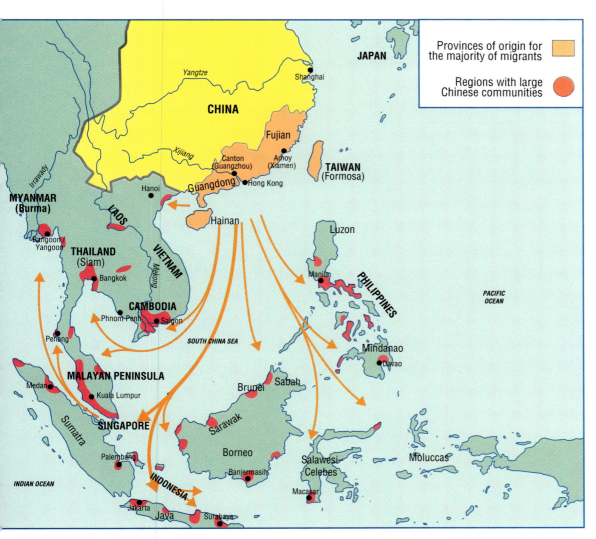

▶ SOUTHEAST ASIA, AN AREA OF
TRADITIONAL CHINESE IMMIGRATION
(14th–19th c.)

The majority of Chinese migrating to
the Philippines, the Malayan peninsula,
Peru, Chile, the West Indies, and California came from the following regions: Hainan, Fukien, Swatow, and
Canton. The Cantonese had the reputa-
tion of being the most enterprising and
were also to be found in Vietnam,
Burma, Hawaii, Indonesia, and Australia.

People from Hainan generally went
to nearby countries: Vietnam, Thailand, Malay Peninsula.

People from Fukien often emigrated
to the Philippines, Taiwan, Vietnam,
Java, and Thailand as well as Australia.

The Hakkas were a distinct group,
most of whom emigrated to Sumatra,
Singapore, and Penang.

THE CHINESE DIASPORA CA. 1910

Hong Kong[1]	444,000
Macao	570,000
Dutch East Indies	1,825,000
Siam	1,500,000
Malay Peninsula (with Singapore)	900,000
French Indochina	250,000
Burma	130,000
Philippines	40,000
British West Indies	80,000
Cuba	10,000
Brazil	20,000
Peru	47,000
United States	133,000
(Hawaii alone)	27,000
Canada	12,000
Australia	25,000
Siberia	37,000

1. According to the *China Yearbook,* no. 1, (Shanghai: Commercial Press, 1924). If Hong Kong and Macao are removed from the list the total number of Chinese outside China is some five million.

It is difficult to estimate the number of Chinese overseas at the beginning of the century. The figures in the table at left, taken from the *China Yearbook,* should be used with caution, some more than others.

According to Dutch colonial sources, in 1917 there were 700,000 Chinese, 300,000 of them in Java, and the rest on the east coast of Sumatra and in Borneo.

The figure for the Malay Peninsula is probably accurate. According to the British authorities, in about 1920 the Chinese population represented 48 percent of the total (2.8 million) and they outnumbered the Malays. The Chinese worked in the tin mines. In the mid-nineteenth century the peninsula was very underpopulated. Under British rule the country experienced considerable development thanks to the tin mines and the rubber plantations. Before the arrival of the British (and East Indian administrator Raffles) Singapore was only a small port with a few hundred Malay fishermen.

The figure given for the British West Indies, even taking into account a high turnover of migrants, is obviously too high. Today the Chinese population in the West Indies, including Cuba, is almost negligible.

Before the Franco-Chinese war of 1884, the Chinese moved freely into Vietnam. At that time there were an estimated 25,000 Chinese in Tonkin and 45,000 in Cochin China.

In 1910 there were 70,000 Chinese in Saigon and Cholon alone and in 1920, 100,000.

In 1874 a Peruvian mission was sent to China to negotiate a treaty for the importation of labor. By 1900, 3 to 5 percent of the Peruvian population was Chinese (no census).

The number of Chinese in Peru increased so much that in 1909 a decree prohibited the entry of Chinese not possessing five hundred pounds sterling. The Chinese government protested and two protocols were signed, but their effect was to put a brake on immigration.

Chinese immigration was also significant in Cuba and in the British West Indies, but the stay was usually only temporary.

The earliest Chinese revolutionary activities directed against the Manchu dynasty, which resulted in the advent of the republic in 1911, were the work of overseas Chinese. Sun Yat-sen himself had emigrated to Hawaii and studied in Hong Kong. The revolutionary movement initially relied on the Chinese in southeast Asia, who were freer and more prosperous. It had the backing of the overseas secret societies.

Later, after the establishment of the republic, a ministry for the overseas Chinese was set up. Consulates were opened in Malaya, the Dutch East Indies, and the Philippines. Only Thailand rejected the opening of diplomatic relations with China, fearing that the new regime might have an excessive influence on the country's Chinese minority. The Kuomintang considered the overseas Chinese—whenever they emigrated—to be full Chinese citizens.

THE CHINESE IN SOUTHEAST ASIA

Estimates, 1989

Vietnam[1]	0.6 million
Thailand	4.0 million
Myanmar (Burma)	0.5 million
Malaysia	6.5 million
Indonesia	4.2 million
Philippines	0.7 million
Other countries	0.9 million

1. There has been a significant exodus since 1979, involving some 250,000 to 300,000 Chinese.

Almost all the Chinese in southeast Asia, even if they started out as farm laborers or mine workers, ended up after one or two generations in towns. The Chinese diaspora is an urban one—as indeed are almost all diasporas.

In southeast Asia today, the Chinese diaspora is approximately twenty million strong (not counting Taiwan and Hong Kong), and there are over two million in the rest of the world. According to the *Nihon Keizai Shimhun* (a Japanese economic newspaper), in Indonesia, where they account for 3 percent of the population, 70 percent of capital is in the hands of Chinese. In the Philippines, 60 percent of the business sector is Chinese (who make up 1 percent of the population).

In 1965 and again in 1970, the Chinese were victims of massacres in Indonesia—their prosperity making them scapegoats.

Macao's Chinese community, 1987 (Photo © P. Zachmann-Magnum). ▲

THE CHINESE IN THE UNITED STATES

Chinese immigration began in 1852. At that time there were eighteen thousand Chinese.[1] By 1860, with the gold rush, this figure had risen to thirty-five thousand. Outside the mines, many worked on the construction of the Central Pacific Railroad and other railways. Others were farm laborers, servants, and laundrymen.

Hostility to the Chinese was strongly expressed in California, where they were competing with white, especially Irish, workers.

In 1852 and 1855 the governor of California protested against Chinese immigration and a tax was imposed on foreign miners.

In 1880 there was a major anti-Chinese riot in Denver.

In 1882 the federal government suspended the immigration of Chinese workers for ten years (Chinese Exclusion Act, 6 May 1882).

In 1892 the Geary Act renewed the exclusion law for ten years.

In 1890 the Chinese population was 107,488.[2]

From then on it fell: 89,863 in 1900, 71,531 in 1910 and, at the time of the 1920 census, 61,639 remaining Chinese, a decline of 45 percent in fifty years. In 1910, out of a total of 71,531, only 4,675 were women.

The overwhelming majority of the Chinese community was on the Pacific coast and 70 percent lived in cities, especially San Francisco, Los Angeles, Seattle, and Portland.

Chinese colonies were established in New York, Philadelphia, and Boston. It was after the restrictions on Chinese immigration that the introduction of Japanese labor began, in 1885.

1. *Bureau of the Census Bulletin*, 127:7 (Washington, D.C.: Department of Commerce, 1852).

2. Ibid. This figure of course does not include Hawaii.

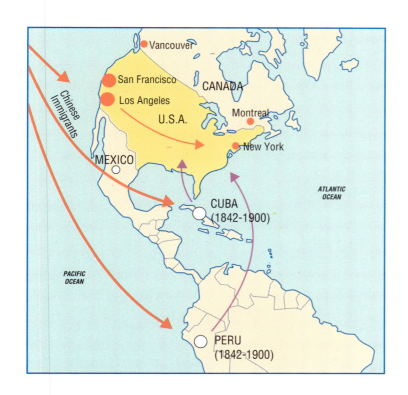

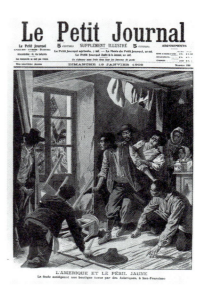

"America and the Yellow Peril," ▲
cover of the *Petit Journal,*
19 January 1909
(Photo © J. Vigne).

◄ CHINESE IMMIGRATION IN THE NEW
WORLD (NINETEENTH CENTURY).

The case of Hawaii is a special one. The islands were annexed in 1898 and from that date, Chinese immigration, which had been significant, was halted. At the 1900 census there were 25,757 Chinese in Hawaii. The application of the Exclusion Acts dates from 1900, and the one relating to the Philippines from 1902, after it had become an American colony (1898).

The Chinese Exclusion Acts were originally aimed solely at Chinese workers but, even before the end of the century, these restrictions were often extended to other Asians.

Interracial marriages between whites and Chinese were explicitly banned in the following states: Arizona, California, Mississippi, Nevada, and Utah (two of these states had almost two thirds of the Chinese in the United States). Interracial marriages were banned in thirty other states at the beginning of the century, but this ban was aimed at black-white unions.

The Chinese minority was foreign by nationality until the Second World War. Over time, the younger generation, born in the United States, became integrated into the American system, notably through the universities. Chinatowns, the most famous being those in San Francisco, New York, and Los Angeles, continue to survive even though English has become the everyday language.

In 1960 there were 200,000 Chinese in the United States; in 1990, 1,260,000.

Chinese butcher's and grocer's shop, Chinatown, San Francisco. (Photo Isaac West Taber, 1887) ▲
(Scottish National Portrait Gallery, Riddell Collection D. R.)

THE CHINESE IN
CANADA

Chinese immigration developed mainly after 1870 on the west coast with the construction of the Canadian Pacific Railway and the gold mines—just as the number of racial clashes in the mines in Australia was rising. In the beginning, immigration was unrestricted. After 1886, a tax of fifty dollars per head was required for entry. Yet the number of Chinese rose from about 10,000 in 1891 to over 16,500 by 1901. In that year the tax was raised to one hundred dollars and in 1904 to five hundred dollars.

This increase halted immigration for three years.

In 1907 there were two days of racial riots in the Asian district of Vancouver.

But at the 1911 census, there were 27,774 Chinese.[1]

In 1913–1914 a law was passed prohibiting the entry of workers. Chinese entered as students until 1923, when a law was passed to restrict the immigration of Chinese businessmen and students.

Chinese immigration has resumed in the last quarter of a century: Montreal, Toronto, and Vancouver now have large Chinatowns. In the last few years wealthy Hong Kong businessmen, worried about the future status of the island, have invested heavily in property in Vancouver.

1. *Statesman's Yearbook*, 1915.

Just as the gold rush attracted Chinese immigrants to the United States, so the discovery of gold in eastern Australia drew Chinese to New South Wales in the 1850s.

Out of a total of 50,000 Chinese leaving only the port of Hong Kong between 1860 and 1866, 37,500 were headed for California and Australia.

Rejection by the host societies was not long in coming. In Australia the parliaments of New South Wales and Victoria imposed a tax of ten pounds sterling payable by each Chinese immigrant on entry between 1855 and 1858. Other parliaments, such as that of Queensland, soon did the same. But the hostility of gold seekers, sailors, and workers in general led to the adoption of the White Australia policy. In 1857 the number of Chinese in the gold mines in Victoria was 26,370, at a time when there were 59,053 whites.

THE CHINESE IN AUSTRALIA

THE SITUATION TODAY

Until the First World War, in the Anglo-Saxon countries (the United States, Canada, and Australia), the qualities of Chinese immigrants—hardworking, sober, active, enterprising, adaptable, and independent—were held against them, as were their large numbers. The Chinese migrant had no rights and did not enjoy the protection of his government. He could count only on his own abilities, his money when he earned it, and the good will of the local authorities. He also had the network of secret societies to which he belonged. But his adaptability was perceived as excessive, his independence deemed antisocial, his family or ethnic network perceived as too exclusive.

The major changes of the last twenty-five years concern the great increase in Chinese emigration to the West: the United States (1,260,000 in 1990), Canada, and Western Europe. A reasonable estimate would put the number of Chinese in all Western countries at at least 2.5 million.

On the other hand, 250,000 to 300,000 Chinese left Vietnam, both North and South, after the Sino-Vietnamese clashes of 1979.

Today, the Chinese diaspora is the biggest in the world and one of the most prosperous.

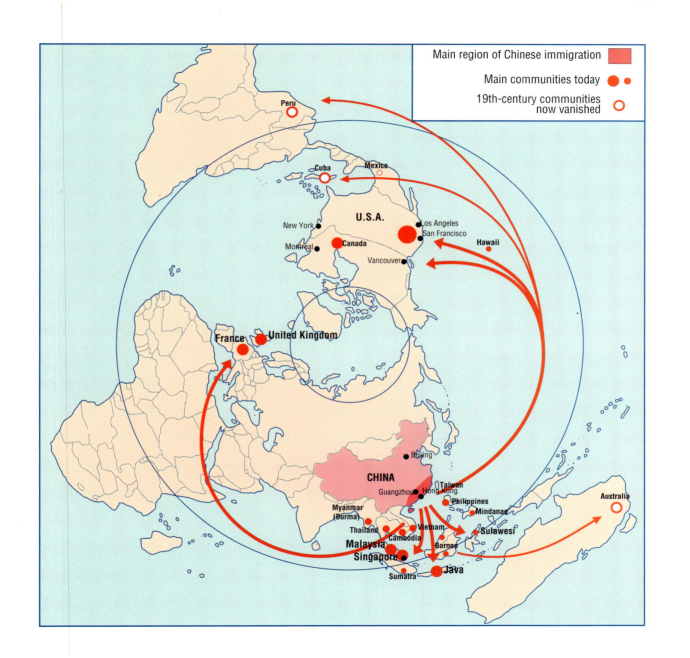

Main region of Chinese immigration

Main communities today ● •

19th-century communities now vanished ○

Peru

Cuba   Mexico

U.S.A.

New York   Los Angeles
San Francisco

Montreal   Canada   Hawaii

Vancouver

France   United Kingdom

Beijing

CHINA

Guangzhou   Hong Kong   Taiwan

Myanmar   Philippines
(Burma)   Mindanao

Thailand   Vietnam   Sulawesi

Cambodia   Australia

Malaysia   Borneo

Singapore   Java

Sumatra

Newsgirl in Capetown, South Africa ▶
(Photo © R. Burri-Magnum).

THE INDIAN DIASPORA

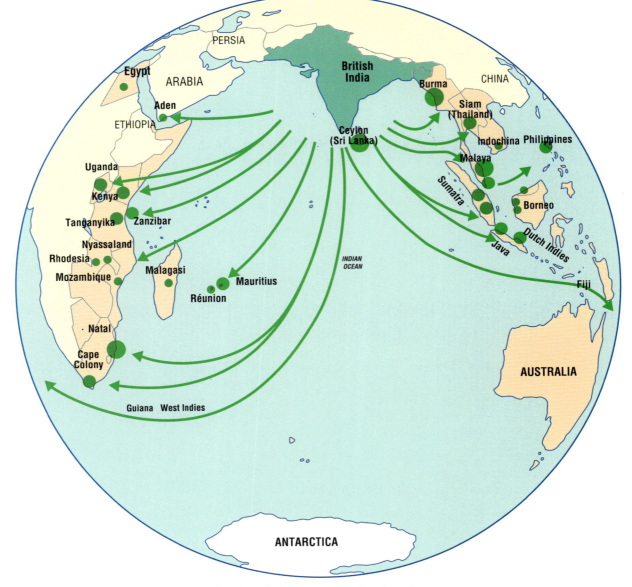

At the time of "British India" the term "Indian" referred to all ethnic groups on the subcontinent.

In the course of the eighteenth and nineteenth centuries Britain built up the centerpiece of its empire in India. In 1947 it withdrew after deciding on partition between Muslims (Pakistan) and Hindus.

Modern Indian emigration originated with the abolition of slavery in 1833 in the British Empire. After a transition period, slaves, in the West Indies and elsewhere, became freemen in 1838. The effect in the islands where the slaves were used on plantations was immediate. In Mauritius, as in the West Indies, depression struck the sugar industry.

Indian emigration, which involved both Hindus and Muslims, who had been present in India since the sixteenth century, began in 1834, first in the Indian Ocean area. Between 1834 and 1837, seven thousand emigrants left Calcutta for Mauritius. Others went to British Guiana (1838), Trinidad (1844), Jamaica (1845), and Natal, in South Africa (1860).

In 1848, slavery was abolished in the French colonies and the planters on Réunion brought in labor from Pondicherry. By 1851 there were twenty-three thousand Indian workers in Réunion. Others went to Guadeloupe and French Guiana.

Conditions on the journey were extremely bad and mortality was high on both British and French boats. Within a few decades, there was a significant Indian presence in Natal (South Africa), Surinam, British Guiana, Trinidad, Réunion and Mauritius, Fiji (South Pacific), etc.

◀ TRANSPORT OF INDIAN WORKERS IN THE NINETEENTH CENTURY

Famines and epidemics in India

	Number of deaths
1837	8,500,000
1861	13,300,000
1866	16,200,000
1874	17,750,000
1877	26,900,000

THE INDIANS IN NORTH AMERICA

1. Among the other dominions, Australia remained closed until after the Second World War.

The indenture system, which was the name given to the type of contract used in this emigration, was based on work hiring for a given period, usually three to five years, in exchange for the price of the passage and a wage. On the expiration of the contract, the migrant worker had the choice of renewing his contract, seeking work in the host country, or returning home at the expense of the host country.

This system, instituted by the British authorities to prevent abuses, was nullified by employers' determination to make people sign contracts for the longest periods at the lowest wages. The emigrants were almost all male. The indenture system lasted until after the First World War.

Around 1900, Indian emigrants, in very small numbers, began to arrive in North America, usually across the Pacific, to San Francisco and Vancouver. Canada[1] received seven thousand Indian migrants between 1900 and 1910.

Most immigrants came from the Punjab. Many of them had been civil servants in the British Empire; the Sikhs, many of whom had been in the police, went to North America via Singapore and Hong Kong.

In the United States, the Indians, like the Chinese and Japanese, worked in railway building, in sawmills, and as farm workers. In 1907 there were a thousand Indians in the United States. Immigration became significant only in the 1970s. By 1990 there were 680,000 Indians in the United States.

Indian, mostly Tamil, emigration to Ceylon (Sri Lanka) dates from very early times and has continued in large numbers down to the present day. At the 1921 census, there were 1,400,000 Indians in Ceylon, almost all Tamils, out of a total population of 5.5 million.

In Burma at the same date, there were over a million Indians out of a total population of thirteen million. In Malaya, after the First World War, there were some 600,000 Indians. Mostly Tamils, the Indians who arrived in the third quarter of the nineteenth century worked in the rubber and sugar cane plantations as in the islands of the Indian Ocean or the West Indies. Indians began to arrive in Borneo (Indonesia) in 1860.

While the Indian diaspora of Tamil origin has maintained itself in Sri Lanka and even carved out a special status by force of arms, most of the Indians in Burma were expelled in the 1960s. In Thailand, Malaya, and Singapore, Indian colonies, often made up of Tamils, are still present, mostly in business. In the Indian Ocean, large colonies exist in Mauritius (over half the total population) and Réunion. The proportion of Indians in Madagascar remains small.

But outside Sri Lanka, Burma, and Malay Peninsula, where Indians were numerous during British colonial rule, the Indian presence has had little impact in southeast Asia since the penetration of Islam into that region of the world in the sixteenth century. At that time the Muslim Mughal dynasty established its dominion over almost the whole of India except for the southernmost tip.

However, the cultural expansion of India in the remote past is still very much a living influence over a large part of southeast Asia, known as

INDIAN EMIGRATION TO SOUTHEAST ASIA

150

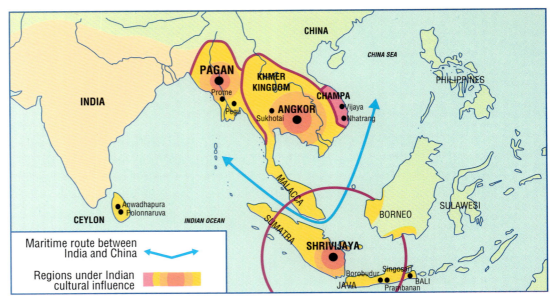

Maritime route between India and China

Regions under Indian cultural influence

HINDU ASIA ▶

CHINA

CHINA SEA

PHILIPPINES

PAGAN

Prome

KHMER KINGDOM

CHAMPA

Vijaya

Nhatrang

INDIA

Pegu

Sukhotai

ANGKOR

MALACCA

SUMATRA

BORNEO

SULAWESI

CEYLON

Anwadhapura

Polonnaruva

INDIAN OCEAN

SHRIVIJAYA

Borobudur

Singosari

BALI

JAVA

Prambanan

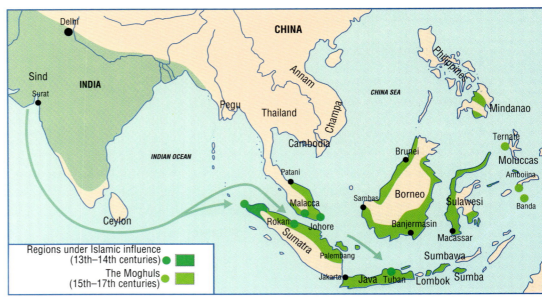

THE ISLAMIZATION OF SOUTHEAST ASIA ▶

Regions under Islamic influence (13th–14th centuries)

The Moghuls (15th–17th centuries)

Delhi

CHINA

Sind

Surat

INDIA

Pegu

Annam

Thailand

Champa

CHINA SEA

Philippines

Mindanao

Cambodia

Ternate

Moluccas

INDIAN OCEAN

Patani

Brunei

Amboiina

Malacca

Sambas

Borneo

Sulawesi

Banda

Ceylon

Rokan

Johore

Banjermasin

Sumatra

Macassar

Palembang

Sumbawa

Jakarta

Java

Tuban

Lombok

Sumba

Hinduized Asia even though Islam has had a profound impact on several formerly Hinduized countries. India's direct or indirect influence through Hinduism and Buddhism is marked in Myanmar (Burma), Thailand, Cambodia, Laos, and Indonesia. In this last country, except in Bali, Islam has established supremacy.

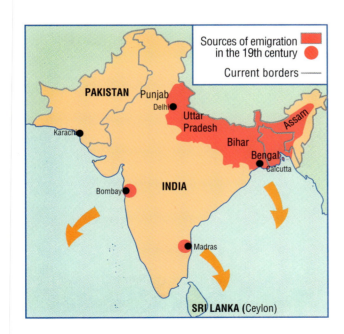

◄ HOME AREAS OF INDIAN EMIGRATION

Estimate of the Indian diaspora on the eve of the Second World War

TOTAL	4 MILLION
Burma[1]	1,100,000
Malaya	750,000
Ceylon	800,000
Mauritius	300,000
South Africa	200,000
Kenya	50,000
Fiji	90,000
Uganda	20,000
Tanganyika	30,000
Zanzibar	8,000
Great Britain[2]	20,000
Indonesia (Dutch East Indies)	35,000
Western Europe	1,000
United States[3]	6,000
West Indies: see table at right	

	Total pop.	Indian pop.	Present since
British Guiana	337,000	150,000	1835
Jamaica	860,000	20,000	1845
Surinam (ex-Dutch Guiana)	165,000	40,000	1873
Trinidad	145,000	110,000	1844
In the Pacific (at the same date)			
Fiji	200,000	85,000	1877

1. Most of the Indians in Burma were expelled in the 1960s.

2. Great Britain today has about 1.5 million Indians, Pakistanis, Bangladeshis, and people from the former Indian empire.

3. The number of Indians in the United States is 680,000 (1990).

INDIANS IN THE WEST INDIES ▶

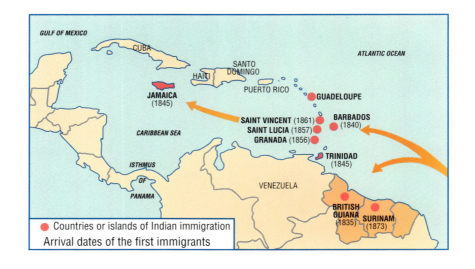

● Countries or islands of Indian immigration
Arrival dates of the first immigrants

It was not until 1910 that the British government introduced laws to put an end to emigration if the host country did not treat its migrants decently. At the time this concerned Natal (South Africa).

In 1911 the government of British India halted emigration to South Africa.

In South Africa itself protest movements appeared—for example the activity of the lawyer Gandhi from 1910 to 1914—to fight against the discrimination and treatment suffered by the Indians. The indenture system introduced in 1860 was challenged. It was in India during 1917 that Gandhi led a massively supported campaign against this system, which was abandoned in 1920.

At that time, in South Africa, out of a total population of 9.6 million, there were only 220,000 Indians. But in Natal there were as many Indians as whites (185,000).

There was a large Indian colony in east Africa and there was also a smaller Indian diaspora in Ethiopia, Somalia, and Madagascar.

In the course of the 1970s a policy of exclusion was imposed on the Indians, especially in Uganda. Most of those in the former British colonies of east Africa who held British passports moved to Britain.

THE INDIANS IN AFRICA

Indians in Africa (1920)

	Kenya	Tanganyika*
Total pop.	3,300,000	5,000,000
Indian pop.	42,000	23,500
European pop.	19,000	9,000
	Uganda	Zanzibar*
Total pop.	3,600,000	138,000
Indian pop.	20,000	15,000
European pop.	2,000	

*Tanganyika and Zanzibar now make up Tanzania.

THE SITUATION TODAY

The Indian diaspora, mostly by the second generation engaged in business, is made up of various ethnic groups (Punjabis, Gujaratis, Bengalis, etc.) and religious ones (Hindus, Muslims, Sikhs, etc.) who all belonged to the British Indian empire. Today it comprises some five or six million people.

Major changes have occurred in recent decades. Local nationalisms have eliminated the Indian trading minorities in Myanmar (Burma) and east Africa, especially Uganda.

Conversely, in Malaysia and Singapore, Sri Lanka, South Africa, Mauritius, Fiji, and the West Indies the Indian communities have put down roots and developed.

Since the sixties, migration has taken many inhabitants of the former Indian empire (Pakistan, Bangladesh, and India) to Britain. They number at least 1.5 million. The United States and Canada have taken in almost 800,000 Indians. And the number of Indians in the European Community is constantly rising. While the poorest social classes are represented, generally speaking, Indians are concentrated in the business sectors.

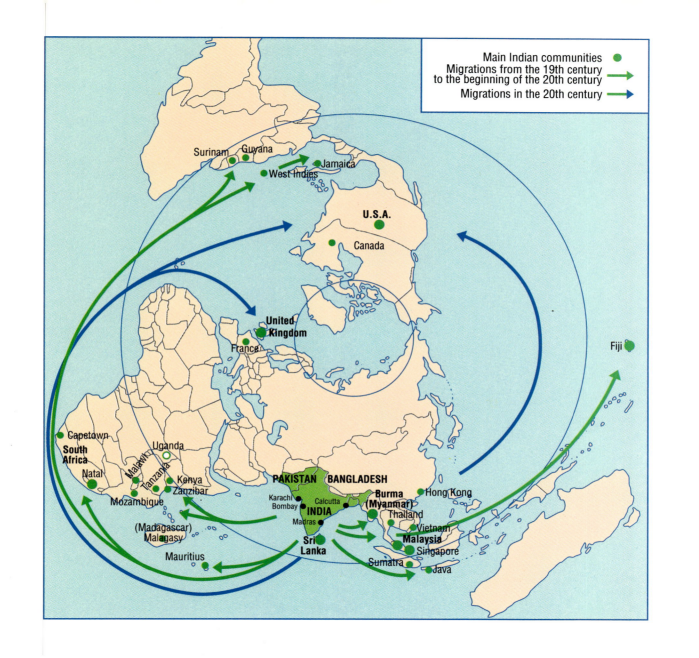

Main Indian communities ●

Migrations from the 19th century to the beginning of the 20th century →

Migrations in the 20th century →

Surinam · Guyana

Jamaica

West Indies

U.S.A.

Canada

United Kingdom

France

Capetown

South Africa

Natal

Uganda

Malawi

Tanzania

Kenya

Zanzibar

Mozambique

(Madagascar) Malagasy

Mauritius

PAKISTAN **BANGLADESH**

Karachi
Bombay

Calcutta

INDIA

Madras

Sri Lanka

Burma (Myanmar)

Hong Kong

Thailand

Vietnam

Malaysia

Singapore

Sumatra

Java

Fiji

THE IRISH DIASPORA

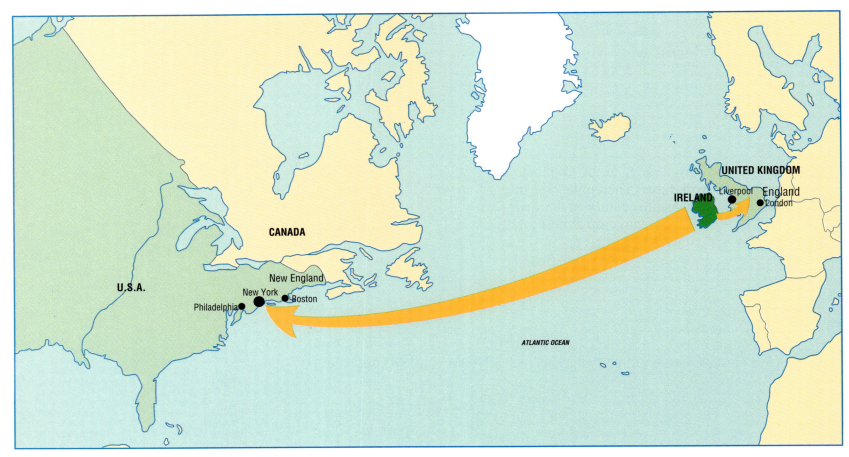

▲ THE GREAT MIGRATION

In 1839, 1 percent of the Irish population made up of landed proprietors owned 80 percent of the arable land in Ireland. Below them, middlemen seeking to make a quick profit let land to workers by the year, very few peasants having enough land to feed their family. By the mid-nineteenth century the Irish agrarian system was particularly archaic, and rents for land were usually exorbitant. Ireland, historically under the thumb of England since the sixteenth century, subsisted thanks mainly to the potato monoculture.

While the population of Ireland rose from 4.2 million in 1800 to 6.5 million in 1845, the situation of the peasantry remained wretched, with no industrialization coming, as in England, to offer an outlet for an underemployed work force. Therein lies the origin of the mass emigration of the Irish in the nineteenth century, in the years following 1840, especially when, in 1846–1847 the potato crop almost totally failed.

They went almost exclusively to the United States, especially between 1840 and 1860. This was the first large wave of non-Protestants that the United States received. A second wave arrived between 1880 and 1890. In total, by 1920, 4.5 million Irishmen had emigrated to the United States.

The population of Ireland fell from 6.5 million in 1840 to about 4 million on the eve of the First World War, despite a high birth rate. This was migration on a scale unparalleled in Europe. It still continues today, although on a far lower scale (30,000 migrants annually between 1985 and 1989).

THE GREAT MIGRATION

THE IRISH-AMERICANS

It may be estimated that there are some twelve million Americans of Irish origin, perhaps more.

Between 1840 and 1860, 1.8 million Irishmen arrived in the United States. This was the biggest arrival of a single population that the United States had experienced and would be equalled between 1880 and 1914 only by the arrival of Jews from Russia and southeastern Europe.[1]

While the famine between 1846 and 1850 killed about one million people, 1.8 million Irishmen reached the United States by way of Liverpool (Ireland, not being independent, was not allowed to have a merchant navy) and settled on the east coast, almost all in urban areas, New York above all, where by 1890 they made up 25 percent of the population. Boston at that time was the second Irish city. Economic conditions were initially extremely precarious and the Irish were the most looked down on of the whites between 1845 and 1885, before the large-scale arrival of immigrants from eastern and southern Europe. There were often bitter conflicts with the Protestant host society. The "papists" were victims of ostracism and denounced as a threat. Many of the railways in the Middle West were built by Irish workers who also provided cheap labor to the factories of the northeast and the coal mines of Pennsylvania. The Irish were numerous and influential in the labor and trade-union world after 1880.

In the United States, Irish migrants, most with rural backgrounds, settled in cities, principally New York, Chicago, Boston, Philadelphia, and San Francisco. On the eve of the First World War, New York City was predominantly Irish and Jewish.

Above all, the Irish diaspora has remained devoted to the Catholic Church

1. Oscar Handlin, *The Uprooted* (Boston, 1951).

which, for its part, has always identified with the Irish cause. The ecclesiastical hierarchy of the Catholic Church in the United States is dominated by clergy of Irish origin; in 1988 there were over fifty-two million Catholics.

The political weight of the Irish within the American Democratic Party has been important all through this century, and the election to the presidency of a Catholic of Irish origin in the person of John F. Kennedy was felt by the Irish community as a victory for the whole group.

The Irish community's sense of cohesion and solidarity remains very much alive, and from 1968 to 1972, Americans of Irish origin showed through large-scale demonstrations their attachment to the cause of Irish unification. Some of the financial aid enjoyed by the militant Catholics in Ulster undoubtedly comes from the Irish community in the United States.

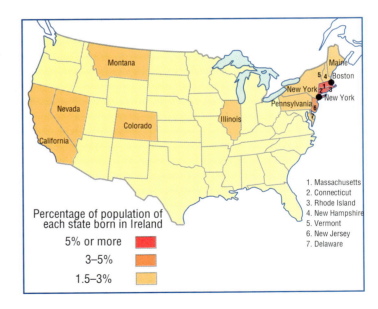

1. Massachusetts
2. Connecticut
3. Rhode Island
4. New Hampshire
5. Vermont
6. New Jersey
7. Delaware

Percentage of population of each state born in Ireland

5% or more

3–5%

1.5–3%

IRISH IMMIGRANTS IN THE UNITED STATES IN 1910 ▶

THE GREEK DIASPORA

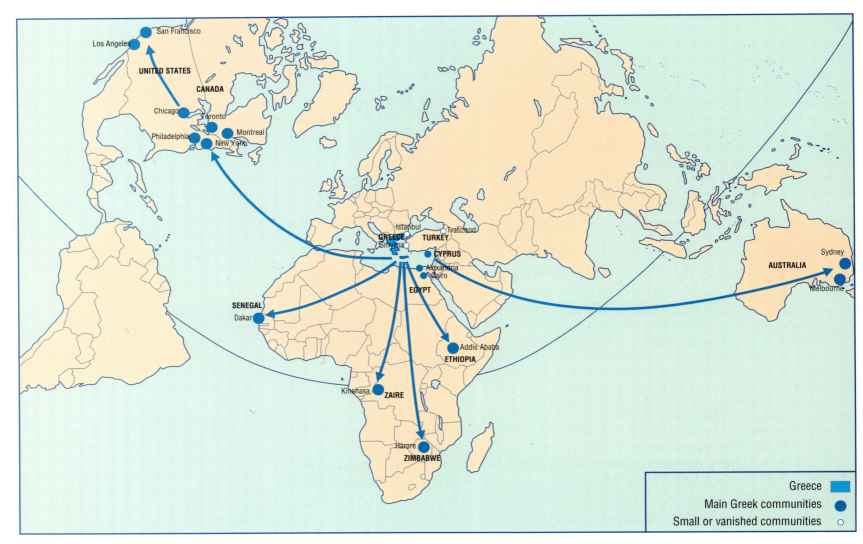

San Francisco
Los Angeles
UNITED STATES
CANADA
Chicago **Toronto**
Philadelphia **Montreal**
New York
Istanbul **Trabzond**
GREECE **TURKEY**
Smyrna
CYPRUS
Alexandria **Cairo**
EGYPT
SENEGAL
Dakar
Addis Ababa
ETHIOPIA
Kinshasa **ZAIRE**
Harare
ZIMBABWE
Sydney
AUSTRALIA
Melbourne

Greece
Main Greek communities
Small or vanished communities

▲ GREEKS IN THE MODERN WORLD

A greek diaspora survived for centuries until quite recently in Asia Minor, Egypt, and the Ottoman Empire in general.

Alexandria was long a Hellenistic center before becoming Muslim, and Asia Minor, along the Black Sea and even more along the Aegean Sea, was Greek. The Greek kingdom of Pontus disappeared in the fifteenth century under the blows delivered by the Ottomans; the Greeks of Pontus disappeared during the First World War through deportations and massacres organized by the Young Turks.

The Greek offensive of 1920–1921, intended to create a Greek state based in Smyrna on the ruins of the Ottoman Empire, was a failure. The victorious troops of Mustafa Kemal (later know as Atatürk) put Smyrna (Izmir) to the torch. In 1922–1923 the decision was taken and implemented to carry out an exchange of populations, whereby Greece took in 1,200,000 expelled Greek Christians and Turkey, 650,000 Turkish Muslims.

In Egypt, the Greek community lived mainly in Cairo and even more Alexandria, the cosmopolitan city described by Lawrence Durrell. It survived in Egypt until the advent of Nasserism and left the country gradually between 1956 and 1962. From then on the Greek community in Egypt was headed for extinction.

A Greek diaspora exists in sub-Saharan Africa, made up of traders, especially in Addis Ababa, where they were numerous up to 1974, when the emperor was deposed. Greeks are present in many towns and cities of central and southern Africa, in Zaire, Zimbabwe, etc.

Large Greek colonies have long been settled in the United States, Canada, and Australia (500,000).

THE TWENTIETH CENTURY

THE LEBANESE DIASPORA

In the second half of the nineteenth century, the mountains of Lebanon, long a region of refuge for persecuted religious minorities, became a land of emigrants.

The core of this emigration was made up of mountain peasants fleeing economic conditions that had become very hard. A small intellectual elite left Lebanon in the second half of the nineteenth century for Egypt and occasionally the United States. The majority of Lebanese went to Latin America, where they were described as *Turcos* (they were Ottoman subjects). Argentina and Brazil were the two main receiving countries. A smaller-scale emigration took them to tropical Africa, from Dakar to southern Africa, in both French-speaking states like the Ivory Coast and Congo and English-speaking ones like Nigeria or Ghana, where Lebanese play a major role in local trade, both wholesale and retail.

Lebanese emigrants also went to the United States and, in smaller numbers, to Australia.

During the period of the French mandate, between the two world wars, the main emigrants were members of the elite who went to Egypt. Following the Second World War, newly independent Lebanon experienced thirty years of rapid economic growth. After the beginning of the civil war in 1975, emigration, still continuing, took various directions: the most skilled went to the Gulf (Kuwait, Emirates, etc.); others to the West in general (United States, Canada, Australia, France).

As the former mandating power, France has been a major receiving country.

This emigration has involved various communities, but more especially

LEBANON ▲

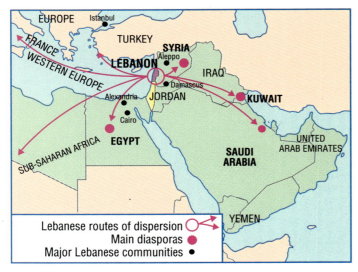

Lebanese routes of dispersion 🔴↗
Main diasporas 🔴
Major Lebanese communities ●

▲ THE LEBANESE IN THE MIDDLE EAST

1. Colin McEvedy and Richard Jones (*Atlas of World Population History*, New York: Penguin, 1979) give the following figures for Lebanon: 1950: 1.5 million; 1975: 3 million. They estimate that 300,000 people emigrated from Lebanon between the nineteenth century and 1975.

the Maronites, Greek Orthodox, and, to a lesser extent, Sunnis.

A distinction must be made between emigration to the Gulf, usually temporary, and black Africa, where assimilation is ruled out, and that to Argentina and Brazil, where the Lebanese have integrated themselves even to the point of losing their language and where, particularly for Christians, one's Lebanese identity is expressed mostly in specific culinary tastes.

The civil war, largely fueled by interference by neighboring states (Syria, Israel, Iran, etc.), will continue to encourage an exodus of Lebanese to more stable countries. It is very risky to venture figures on the population in a country which, for political reasons, has not held any census for half a century. The whole worldwide Lebanese diaspora might number 2.5 million, which would be more or less the same figure as the current Lebanese population.[1]

In the Ivory Coast, the Lebanese trading diaspora has recently been the scapegoat for the country's economic difficulties.

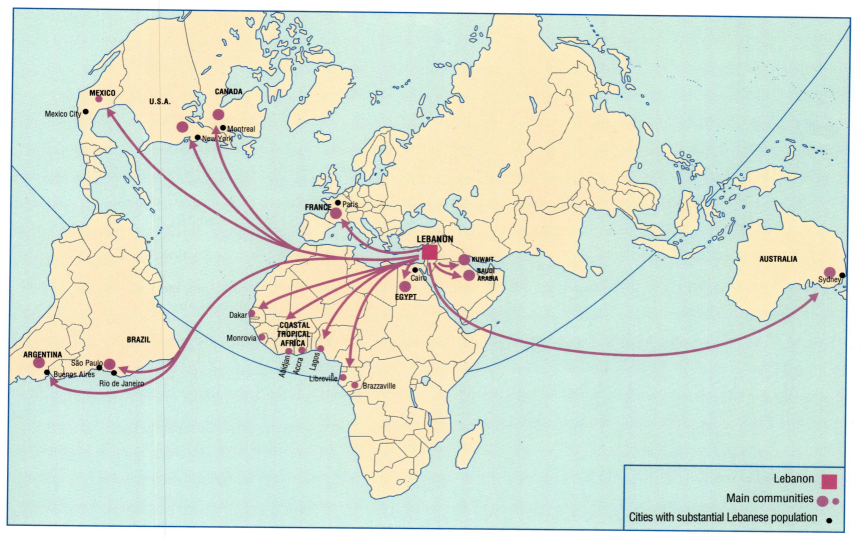

MEXICO
Mexico City

U.S.A.

CANADA
Montreal
New York

FRANCE Paris

LEBANON

KUWAIT
SAUDI ARABIA

Cairo

EGYPT

AUSTRALIA

Sydney

Dakar

Monrovia

COASTAL TROPICAL AFRICA

Abidjan
Accra
Lagos
Libreville
Brazzaville

BRAZIL

ARGENTINA
São Paulo
Buenos Aires
Rio de Janeiro

Lebanon
Main communities
Cities with substantial Lebanese population

THE LEBANESE IN THE MODERN WORLD ▲

▲ A boys' school for refugees in Jordan, 1948 (Photo. © G. Rodgers-Magnum).

THE PALESTINIAN
DIASPORA

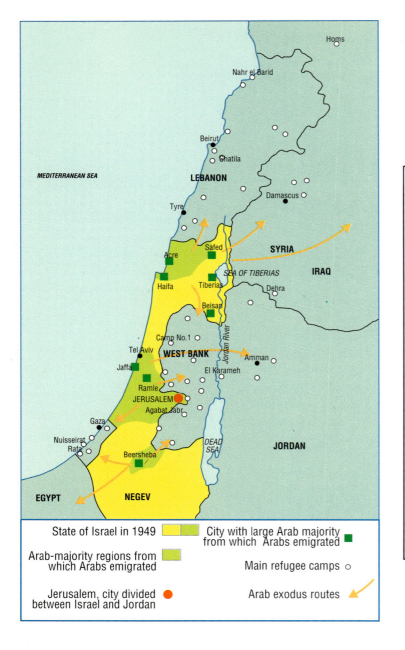

Arab-Israeli Wars

29 November 1947: U.N. plan to partition Palestine rejected by the Arabs.

14 May 1948: British leave; founding of the state of Israel, at once attacked by the bordering states.

9–19 July 1949: "Ten-day campaign," Israel drives the Arab armies back.

October: Israelis occupy the Negev. Cease-fire and establishment of borders.

July 1956: Egypt nationalizes the Suez Canal.

24 October: "Lightning war" by the Israelis, backed by France and Britain, who attack Port Said.

November: U.N. forces the belligerents to withdraw to the 1949 armistice line. U.N. forces guard Sinai.

19 May 1967: Withdrawal of U.N. forces from Sinai.

5 June: Faced with the dispatch of troops from various Arab states to its borders, Israel launches armed conflict.

10 June: Cease-fire. Israel occupies Sinai, Gaza, the West Bank, and the Golan Heights.

6 October 1973: Egypt launches the "October War."

23 October: The U.N. calls for a cease-fire which involves the dispatch of U.N. forces.

◄ PALESTINIAN REFUGEES AFTER THE 1949 ARAB-ISRAELI WAR

The creation of the state of Israel and the upheaval of the 1948–1949 Arab-Israeli War were the origin of the dispersion of part of the Arab population of Palestine.

On 30 June 1948, the Special Office set up by the United Nations to manage the problem of Palestinian refugees (U.N.R.W.A.) carried out a census of them, and counted 900,000. This figure includes the refugees in the West Bank and Gaza. The former of these territories was annexed by the Hashemite dynasty to Transjordan to form the kingdom of Jordan, while Gaza was placed under Egyptian administration.

The territories of Gaza and the West Bank were under Arab administration for almost twenty years. Of the five million Palestinians, a sizable number are refugees with various statuses.

The majority of Palestinians who are neither in Israel proper nor in the West Bank are in the immediate periphery of historic Palestine: Jordan, Lebanon, Syria. In reality at least two thirds of the Jordanian population is made up of Palestinians, many of them with a Jordanian passport.

Apart from those in Gaza and the West Bank, the refugee camps are in Jordan, Lebanon, and Syria.

Palestinian colonies, largely made up of skilled manpower, work in the Gulf, Kuwait, the United Arab Emirates, and Saudi Arabia.

A Palestinian diaspora has also emerged in the United States. Older, well-integrated colonies of Palestinians have also been settled in Chile, Argentina, and Brazil since the second half of the nineteenth century.

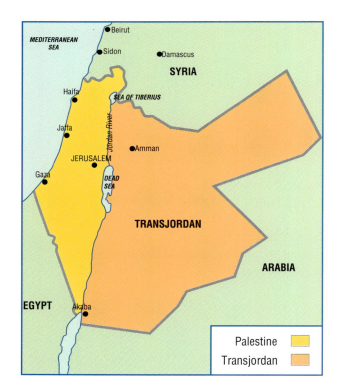

▲ Palestine under British mandate

Great Britain, the mandating power after the collapse of the
Ottoman Empire, placed a Hashemite ruler on the throne of
Transjordan. Historic Palestine remained under mandate until
1947–1948.

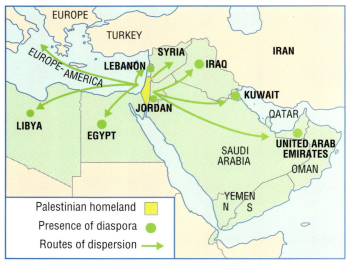

▲ Palestinians in the Near East

Palestinians (1988 estimate)

Israel	600,000		*Other Arab countries:*		
West Bank	980,000	40%	Gulf countries (total)		600,000
Gaza	540,000		Kuwait		360,000
Adjacent countries:			Saudi Arabia		180,000
Jordan	1,380,000	26%	United Arab		
Lebanon	500,000		Emirates		40,000
Syria	260,000	14%	Qatar		30,000
Egypt	40,000		Iraq		25,000
Total Palestinians in			Libya		20,000
historic Palestine and			*United States*		100,000
adjacent countries	4,300,000	80%	*Other countries*		100,000?

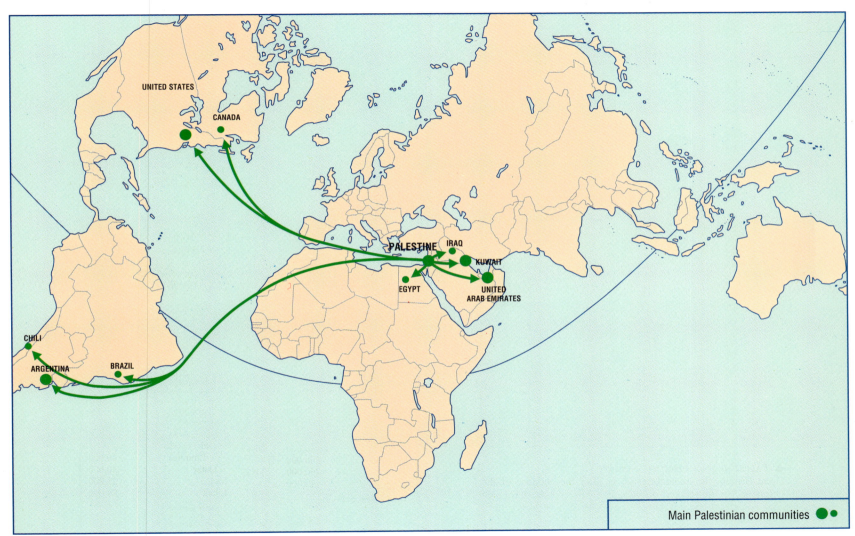

UNITED STATES

CANADA

PALESTINE

IRAQ

KUWAIT

EGYPT

UNITED
ARAB EMIRATES

CHILI

ARGENTINA

BRAZIL

Main Palestinian communities

THE KOREAN AND
VIETNAMESE DIASPORAS

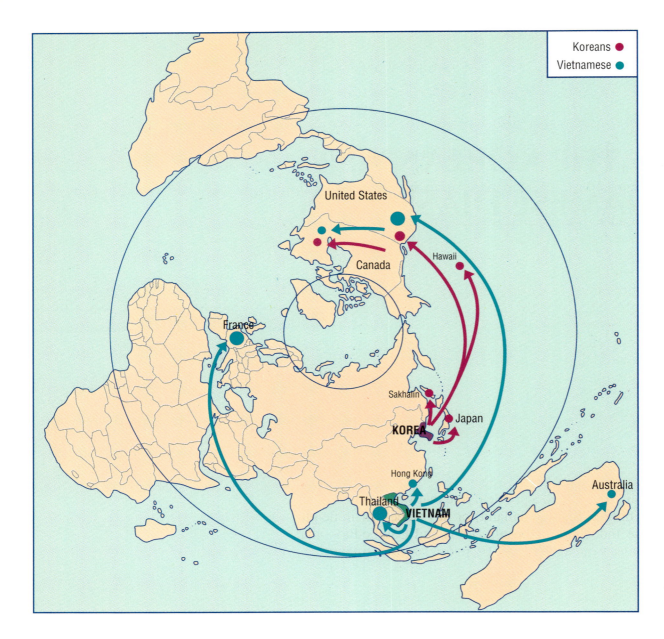

Koreans ●
Vietnamese ●

United States

Canada

Hawaii

France

Sakhalin

Japan

KOREA

Hong Kong

Thailand

VIETNAM

Australia

◀ THE KOREANS AND
VIETNAMESE IN THE
MODERN WORLD

Few people from Korea, strongly rooted in the land, had left the country before Japanese colonization in 1910. It was during this colonial period (1910–1945) that Korean workers settled in Manchuria, Sakhalin, and Japan itself. The inferior status imposed on them in Japan, even after three generations—despite significant improvements—remains obvious. Intermarriage is rare. Following the war, the Soviet hold on Sakhalin prevented any possible return movement by the Korean minority, and others remained in Siberia, on the border with Manchuria.

After 1975, and increasingly in the 1980s, almost half a million South Koreans moved to California, especially Los Angeles.

The Vietnamese diaspora refers to those who left their country after April 1975. It is the product of the conditions that have prevailed in Vietnam at least until 1990, with the flight of those who had worked closely with the Americans on the eve of the fall of Saigon and the clandestine exodus of refugees by sea, accelerating after 1978—when the least appropriate economic measures (general nationalization) were adopted to get the country going again. A bureaucracy that had won the war was trying hard, through sheer dogmatism, to lose the peace.

Before 1945 Vietnamese emigrants in Japan, China, and France, often anti-colonialist in inspiration, played a political role that was essentially intellectual. It was then only in Siam (Thailand) or in France—or in neighboring countries in the Indochina peninsula (Laos and Cambodia)—that large Vietnamese colonies were to be found. By mutual agreement between Bangkok and Hanoi, some of the Vietnamese in Thailand were repatriated

THE KOREANS

THE VIETNAMESE

Vietnamese outside Vietnam*
1975–1990

United States	860,000
Canada	120,000
France	120,000
Australia	120,000
West Germany	24,000
Great Britain	18,000
Other western countries	45,000
Japan	2,700
Estimated total	ca. 1,300,000

*It is estimated that at least 200,000 Chinese from northern Vietnam moved to China after the beginning of the Sino-Vietnamese conflict in 1979. A large number of Chinese also left southern Vietnam between 1978 and 1984.

in 1960. Similarly, several thousand Vietnamese contract workers in New Caledonia were repatriated to North Vietnam in the early 1960s, and adapted to it badly.

In March–April 1975, almost 200,000 Vietnamese sought refuge in the United States and other countries. Compared to this initial departure, the exodus was modest until April 1978: a few hundred per month. After collectivization measures and suppression of the market economy, there were a thousand refugees by sea a month. During the period when departures were greatest, between 1978 and 1985, the U.N. High Commission for Refugees put the figure at half a million. To those figures must be added the legal departures: 30,000 for 1984. But the exodus continued from 1985 to 1990, albeit on a lesser scale. Today, the Vietnamese diaspora is estimated to number 1.3 million, 70 percent of them in the United States.

France, Canada, Australia, Great Britain, and West Germany were among the main receiving countries. This diaspora is largely composed of educated and skilled people, sometimes highly so, and people have immediately secured relatively good positions in both the professions and in business.

"Boat people" off Hong Kong. Since 1978, thousands of Vietnamese have run away from their country in crude boats; Hong Kong has been ▲ turning them away as illegal immigrants since 1988 (Photo © J. Griffiths-Magnum).

DATE DUE

MAY 18 2006		

Demco, Inc. 38-293